PERSUASIVE
THOUGHTS

Silva
UltraMind
SYSTEMS

PERSUASIVE
THOUGHTS
HAVE MORE CONFIDENCE,
CHARISMA, & INFLUENCE

JOSÉ SILVA JR.
KATHERINE SANDUSKY
ED BERND JR.

Foreword by Clancy D. McKenzie, MD

MEDIA

Published 2019 by Gildan Media LLC
aka G&D Media
www.GandDmedia.com

First Edition: 2019

Front Cover design by David Rheinhardt of Pyrographx

Interior design by Meghan Day Healey of Story Horse, LLC.

Library of Congress Cataloging-in-Publication Data
is available upon request

ISBN: 978-1-7225-1012-1

Manufactured in the United States of America by LSC Communications

10   9   8   7   6   5   4   3   2   1

Contents

Part Three
Guiding Principles

Part Four
How to Influence Others

Foreword

by Clancy D. McKenzie MD

When I first took the Silva Mind Control course in 1969, I realized that it was something special and that it could be of great value both to me and to the psychiatric patients I was treating.

The "programmed dreams" technique that is part of the course soon evolved as the most useful technique both for me personally and for my patients.

Insights gained from the programmed dreams proved their value time and again as I began to treat many returning Vietnam veterans who were coming home with what is now called posttraumatic stress disorder (PTSD). Their own interpretation of their programmed dreams gave each one precisely what he needed to solve his own problem.

This was so valuable that when José Silva invited me to be a consultant to him and the Silva organization, I felt honored for the opportunity, because it would be a way for me to give back and help many more people.

Using insights that I gained with the Silva techniques, I found a simple way to determine the origin of depression and schizophrenia, and thousands of patients have benefitted from this discovery.

When we are able to determine when the traumatic event occurred, then we can identify it and treat it.

In this book you will learn exactly how to use this discovery to help you determine the precise origin of any impediment that you feel is holding you back from achieving the success that you know you are capable of—the kind of success enjoyed by other people who are no more talented or hard-working than you are.

A Beautiful Mind

The first time I met John Nash, the Nobel Prize–winning mathematician featured in the movie *A Beautiful Mind,* I told him that the origin of his psychiatric disorder was when he was between fifteen and sixteen months old.

Then Nash informed me that he was sixteen months old in October 1929. That's when the stock market crashed, and people who had invested heavily, especially with borrowed money, were wiped out financially. Many people were so distraught they were jumping off rooftops. Mothers were so upset that their babies felt abandoned.

Schizophrenia and depression are just delayed posttraumatic stress disorders from infancy. The onset of Nash's schizophrenia came when he was in college and a woman he was attracted to rejected him.

A separation from mother trauma during infancy is more overwhelming than war trauma is to a soldier. Later, a separation from a girlfriend or boyfriend can precipitate a flashback to the earlier time, and the individual shifts back to the mind, reality, feelings, behavior, chemistry, physiology, body movements, level of affective expression, and anatomic sites in their brain that were active and developing in that precise moment of time.

It is the same process as acute PTSD. Instead of a loud noise, it is a separation from some other "most important person" that precipitates the initial step back in time. When that happens, the person shifts to using the area of brain that they were using at that age.

Help Is at Hand

In the second week of this 30-day Silva UltraMind Persuasive Thoughts System, you will learn the techniques that I use, and how to apply them, in order to help you recognize the origin of your fears, phobias, and other impediments and how to overcome them.

José Silva was a remarkable man, and I have been honored to serve as a consultant to his organization since 1970. He was in direct communication with the Lord, or as he referred to it, "higher intelligence."

It is really interesting how much higher intelligence wants to help. It took me a while to recognize who was helping. Programmed dreams are one kind of direct connection with that higher power.

When José Silva developed the MentalVideo technique and created the UltraMind ESP System to showcase it and teach it to people, it represented the answer to a question he had sought for at least a quarter of a century.

A Message to Fellow Scientists

"We are interested: Is there a higher intelligence somewhere?" José told a group of fifty scientists in 1973. "Of course we are. We think we are tapping into it at some level, somehow, because we ourselves cannot explain—even ourselves within the movement cannot explain the success that we have had, except through help from higher levels.

"And that is putting it lightly.

"Now our interest would be: Can we establish a better communication with higher levels of intelligence, wherever they are? Are they somewhere in the universe? Are they somewhere in the center of our galaxy? Can we, or should we, communicate subjectively, instead of the way we have been trying before?

"Now there are glimpses and hints in this direction that this could be. It could be. That's a little too far out for most people. Well, we want to research that, even though it may seem so far out, because we are far-out people."

In this book you will learn José Silva's MentalVideo Technique for communicating reliably and regularly with higher intelligence.

You will also learn how I use programmed dreams for myself and for my patients to gain insights that are filed in the deep recesses of our subconscious. You will also learn how to use those dreams and also the new MentalVideo technique to obtain the kind of help from higher intelligence that guided José Silva and me to make breakthroughs that have helped millions of people worldwide to change their lives for the better.

One of the world's foremost experts on schizophrenia and mental health, Dr. McKenzie is the author of two breakthrough books: Delayed Posttraumatic Stress Disorders From Infancy *(with Dr. Lance Wright; Harwood Academic Publishers), and* Babies Need Mothers: How Mothers Can Prevent Mental Illness in Their Children *(Xlibris). He is the founder and director of the Alternative American Psychiatric Association (www.AlternativeAPA.com) for individuals seeking an alternative understanding of the causes of and treatments for mental and emotional disorders.*

Preface

The Life of José Silva

If you want to know that people have the ability to overcome adversity—no matter how early in life or how late or how often it comes—José Silva's life is evidence of that. The lessons that he learned along the way guided him to develop techniques to help his children and eventually millions of other people all over the world.

José Silva was born in Laredo, Texas, in 1914. When he was just four years old, young José saw his father die as the result of a terrorist act during the Mexican revolution. His mother remarried and moved away, so when he found himself the oldest male in his family at the age of six, instead of starting school, young José started work shining shoes.

Although he never attended school as a student, he got an education from a variety of sources that proved to be very valuable both to him and to humanity.

His work on the streets of Laredo taught him the value of honesty and of doing more than people expected from him. He never wanted to gain at somebody else's loss, but only while also helping the other person to gain.

José's curiosity and willingness to ask questions led him to many opportunities. One of those opportunities came when he was fourteen years old. The year was 1928. He had his own business selling household goods door-to-door, and had recruited other youngsters to help him. His sister and younger brother had taught him how to read and write, and he would practice by reading comic books. The pictures helped him understand what the characters were saying.

One afternoon José went to a local barbershop to practice his reading and found a new publication: a correspondence course in radio repair. He asked if he could borrow it, but the barber told him he would rent it to him for one dollar a lesson. That was a lot of money, but José was earning enough that he could easily afford it.

As a result, José got in on the ground floor of a brand-new field just as the Great Depression was forcing millions of Americans out of work. Guided by his intuition and his ability to somehow sense the right things to say and to do, which he had honed on the streets of Laredo, he earned a lot of money. He got married and began to raise a family.

But in 1944 that all came to an abrupt end when José received a notice that he had been drafted to serve in World War II. Not knowing whether he would survive to return home, he liquidated his business and left cash for his family.

It was during the army induction process that José had his first encounter with a psychiatrist. His curiosity about this subject led him to the study of psychology.

After his discharge from the army at the end of the war, he returned to Laredo and started his radio repair business all over again.

He continued to study psychology in hopes of finding ways to help his children use more of their minds so they would get better grades in school. But psychologists had abandoned the study of the mind because they couldn't detect it. Instead they studied behavior.

Some psychologists had also used hypnosis, so José also tried that. He was an excellent hypnotist, and he realized that this was a good way to learn what the mind can do. When he read about a new electronic device called an electroencephalograph—EEG for short—that could detect and measure electrical energy radiating from the brain, he bought one.

He had obtained the kind of education and experiences that no other scientist had:

- His study of psychology taught him about human behavior.
- His experiences with hypnosis showed him what the human mind is capable of doing.
- The electroencephalograph gave him the ability to see what was going on inside a person's head and relate brain activity to mental function.
- In addition, he was a classically trained singer, and his knowledge of music and frequencies and harmonics revealed to him that scientists needed to rethink the way they had been classifying the brain frequency spectrum.

When his neighbors in Laredo saw how much his discoveries were helping his children, they asked José to help their children too. Eventually the adults also wanted to learn his system. Word continued to spread, and eventually he was teaching seminars and training others to also teach his system throughout the United States and around the world.

He held no academic degrees, but received the kind of degree that you cannot get by taking tests in a classroom: a doctor of humanities degree from the Sangreal Foundation, awarded for his life's work, which is the true test of greatness.

This man with no formal schooling wrote the book on the development of mind power—in fact, he's had more than a dozen books published by major publishers, in two dozen languages.

While José Silva may have moved on to new assignments (he passed on in 1999), his work is still going strong, both in live seminars and in convenient home-study courses, and in books like this one.

There are many courses that are "based on" his work, but the only courses still being taught that he authored himself, based on his twenty-two years of scientific research, are the Silva Ultra-Mind ESP System and his Holistic Faith Healing System.

This young boy who started helping people one shoe at a time went on to help millions, not to just look better on the outside, but to actually be better on the inside.

José Silva is a glowing example of what people can achieve no matter how humble their beginnings. This book is the result of his own life experience, along with his pioneering research into how to overcome adversity, gain self-confidence, eliminate fears and phobias, become a more powerful communicator, and develop greater ability to influence yourself and others.

Those traits already live in each of us. When you apply the techniques in this book to bring them forth, and then use them for constructive and creative purposes that will improve living conditions for yourself and others, you will enjoy the kind of success that you know deep within yourself that you are capable of.

Introduction

The greatest discovery you'll ever make is the potential of your own mind.
—JOSÉ SILVA

In this book you will learn how to use your mind power to program yourself for the kind of success that you deserve. It doesn't matter what kind of problems you have now, or may have had in the past.

You will learn how to convert fear into courage and convert doubt into action, to dissolve problems by manifesting solutions, and develop a charisma that radiates out and influences everyone and everything in your life.

Everybody has problems. There is no shortage of books and courses that tell you how to solve your problems. Why so many? Because most of them don't work very well.

You don't solve a problem by trying to solve the problem.

Solving the problem *is* the problem.

Trying to work your way through the problem is like trying to push a strand of cooked spaghetti from the rear: it just gets tangled up into a big sticky mess.

The way to overcome a problem is to leapfrog over the problem, set your sights *beyond* it, and concentrate on a solution.

Take money, for instance. If you don't have enough money to pay your bills, that's a problem, and every time you think about how you can get enough money to pay your bills, you are thinking about the problem.

Mind guides brain and brain guides body, so guess what you are reinforcing.

When you leapfrog over the problem and start thinking about what you can do that has value to someone, then you are doing something that will lead you to the solution.

You do it without working on the problem—you work on the solution.

Unleash Your Hidden Mind Power

José Silva Jr.'s Thirty-Day Plan shows you how to use the untapped power of your mind to banish irrational fears and phobias, and overcome childhood traumas and negative belief systems. It will enable you to develop charisma and confidence and learn to use your mind to become a powerful, persuasive, and effective communicator. You will be able to influence the people and events in your life in a positive way, not only by what you say and do, but also with your personal power.

This book is filled with examples and step-by-step guidance to help you solve many of the most common problems that we encounter—with finances, family, relationships, and health. It will give you the ability to achieve the things that you know deep within yourself that you are capable of achieving.

Discover how your hidden mind power can give you confidence and make you a persuasive, effective, compelling communicator.

Your power to persuade can help you get the job of your dreams.

Your confidence and charisma can attract your ideal mate to find you and want to be with you forever.

You will have the ability to make a good first impression.

As a parent, you can use your hidden persuasive powers to guide and protect your children from infancy through childhood and the teenage years and into adulthood.

All great leaders have been able to communicate their vision by the power of their presence. You can do even more than inspire people with your confidence: you can instill your confidence in them, and by doing that you will magnify its effectiveness many times over.

Develop Confidence and Charisma

Have you ever wondered why some people seem "bigger than life"? Their physical bodies might even be small, but they some-how seem to occupy more space and have greater impact and influence than most people.

They don't influence others by pushing their ideas at them. They get out in front and project ideas and solutions that inspire us. Their shared ideals become our own ideals, because these leaders have the ability to project mentally to where we are and influence us.

In this book we will reveal what our scientific research has dis-covered about how leaders are able to motivate us so much more effectively than the average person can. More importantly, we will show you how to do what they do.

If you are ready to overcome irrational fears and self-doubt and old limiting beliefs, and replace them with confidence and charisma and genuine optimism that will produce a powerful and positive influence on the people and circumstances in your life, now is the time to do it.

What to Expect during the Next Thirty Days

There are fifteen lessons in this book, with two days to practice each lesson. Just do the lessons in order and follow the instructions, and you will succeed.

Here is what you can expect when you follow the simple step-by-step instructions:

Week 1: As you practice entering the alpha brain-wave level by practicing the Silva Centering Exercise, you will feel more relaxed and less tense, more energetic, optimistic, and hopeful. Notice how this affects you:

- You will find it easier to get up in the morning and greet the new day.
- Your work will go a little more smoothly because you are more relaxed and optimistic, and because you are beginning to take advantage of the powerful alpha levels, where there is more information you can use to help you make better decisions.
- You will find it easier to fall asleep at night.

In chapter 2 you will learn the truth about positive thinking, and why much of what people say about it is wrong. We provide specific guidance to help you keep your thoughts positive, and will show you how to convert negative thoughts into positive ones.

As you begin to use more positive words and ideas when you communicate with people, they will respond better to you, because you will be projecting a more relaxed and optimistic attitude that will make them feel good about you and about themselves.

This new attitude will help you get more things accomplished, because you will feel better, and people around you will also feel better. This will be beneficial in your work, your family, and your social life.

In chapter 3 you will go far beyond the use of positive words and phrases, and begin to communicate with yourself and with others using the universal language that everybody understands: visualization and imagination.

You will be amazed at how much easier it is to understand what other people are saying, and how much easier it is to communicate your ideas clearly to others when you incorporate conscious visualization and imagination into your thinking and your communication with others.

In chapter 4 you will learn specific techniques for incorporating your positive thinking, as well as your visualization and imagination, in order to program yourself for success.

You will also discover what José Silva learned in his twenty-two years of scientific research about the secret thought process that all truly successful people use.

Week 2: In chapter 5 you will learn how to overcome fears and phobias, relieve guilt, banish doubt, and change them to courage, self-esteem, and self-confidence.

You will learn how to neutralize negative past traumas and old limiting belief systems.

You will learn how to eliminate fears and phobias, such as the fear of public speaking, fear of failure, fear of success, and learn to welcome new challenges with the confidence that you can handle them and use them to help you succeed.

Chapter 6 will take a look at how to use your inner conscious level to help heal "the wounded child within." We will approach the problem from several different directions at once in order to bring about a solution.

Chapter 7 will guide you with special techniques for stopping bad habits that are inhibiting you and starting good new habits that will help to automatically propel you to greater achievements.

Chapter 8 shows you how to program to overcome health problems and to help you maintain a perfectly healthy body. This will ensure that you will have the energy to do whatever you need to do to fulfill your special mission in life.

When you remove these impediments to your success, you will notice that you feel better about yourself, your work will benefit, people will respond to you in a more positive way, and you will accomplish more than before.

Week 3: In chapter 9 you will learn a special technique that José Silva developed shortly before his passing after more than fifty years of scientific research and experience in the mind training field. This is a scientific way to communicate reliably and regularly with higher intelligence in order to obtain guidance and support for solving problems and improving living conditions on planet earth.

In chapter 10 you will learn the five Laws of Programming that José Silva developed using his scientific research about successful people and how they differ from average people.

You can have the full power of higher intelligence working for you, provided that you are doing what this higher power wants you to do. The Laws of Programming will help you to continue moving in the right direction.

You will learn how to incorporate these five laws into your life immediately in order to bring you benefits and advantages that you desire in all areas of your life.

Chapter 11 takes a scientific look at faith. It also describes specific techniques to help you increase your desire and motivation to achieve, your belief in yourself, and your expectation to succeed.

Those are the three elements of faith—desire, belief, and expectation. You will learn what José Silva discovered when he applied his scientific approach to the subject of faith.

Using these techniques will supercharge your programming and help you achieve greater success faster than before.

Week 4: During the previous three weeks you will have practiced using your mind the way ultrasuccessful people do. You will have begun neutralizing impediments to your success, and you will now know how to use visualization and imagination in order to help you solve problems and improve living conditions on the planet.

Now we will turn our attention to advanced techniques, and specialized applications of your newly learned skills.

In chapter 12 you will learn how to use your aura to help you detect information and to communicate your thoughts more effectively and persuasively.

Everybody knows about the so-called five physical senses. We now know that there are more than five. Have you ever stared at somebody, at the back of their head perhaps, and found that eventually they turn and look at you? Or perhaps you are the one who was stared at, and you detected it.

That happens with the physical part of your aura. Your body radiates energy, both physical and nonphysical energy. When you know what to do, you can use the physical part of your aura to influence people who are in the vicinity.

They might also be influencing you, whether they know it or not. Have you ever started to feel nervous and not known why? It could be that you are detecting someone else's mood through aura transmission.

It is easy to control what you transmit and what you receive through the aura—once you understand how it works and know what to do.

This ability can help you make a good first impression, improve your relationships, and even help you detect what other people are thinking and feeling.

It is not just humans who are affected by the radiation of your aura. Everything in the vicinity is impressed with information that is transmitted automatically by your aura. There are many ways in which this can be beneficial to you.

Chapter 13 is about what is probably your most important relationship: with your family. José and Paula Silva were married for sixty years and had ten children, so they learned a lot about family relationships. They share their knowledge in this chapter.

Chapter 14 continues with more techniques and more ways to use your persuasive thoughts to help you in your business and personal life.

Chapter 15 brings it all together in what we call *a new way of living*. Not using your mind is like not using one of your legs—it puts you at a big disadvantage. That is why we finish with specific guidance about how to easily and naturally incorporate what you have learned into your daily life so that you use it automatically, without even having to think about it, the way ultrasuccessful people do.

If you are willing to follow the simple instructions and complete this thirty-day program, and then continue to practice what you have learned, you will succeed.

How You Will Benefit

We all have problems, and trying to unravel them and push our way through them usually doesn't work very well.

In this book you will learn how to move past your problems and focus on solutions.

We all admire the great communicators and great persuaders, and wonder if they have some secret or some special skill.

The truth is that 10 percent of people do use more of their minds than the average person, and use it in a special way.

You are just moments away from learning what their secret is, and over the next thirty days you will learn exactly how to use your mind the way ultrasuccessful people do.

If you want to unleash your superpowers and use them to solve more problems and improve living conditions for yourself and others—and if you are willing to practice and to invest as little as fifteen minutes a day—you too are just thirty days away from joining the 10 percent who use their superpowers naturally.

In fact you will be able to do more than the ultrasuccessful people do, because you will know why they are so successful, and you will know exactly how to use your powers.

Be Ready to Claim Your Rewards

Join the millions of people worldwide who have benefited from José Silva's scientifically researched techniques over the last fifty years and use this Thirty-Day Plan developed by José Silva Jr. to help you think, talk, act, and unleash the superpowers that already reside within you.

Once you have completed this Thirty-Day Plan to develop your own inner strength, the techniques that you have read about and heard about from supersuccessful people will work for you too, because you will be using your brain and mind the way that they use theirs.

Meet the Authors

José Silva Jr. was the first of José and Paula Silva's ten children. He was there when his father began the scientific research that unlocked the secret of developing intuition and using it regularly and reliably in all aspects of your life.

Nobody is more qualified than Joe Jr., as we call him, to teach you how to apply his father's research findings to your business career.

Joe was not a research subject. He documented the research that his father conducted with his brothers and sisters, recording the sessions with an old Roberts reel-to-reel tape recorder, and filing the data that his father was acquiring.

While his younger sisters and brothers were sitting with their eyes closed following their father's instructions, Joe was observing and recording the whole process, providing him with a unique understanding of how to how to help the average person develop extraordinary mental powers.

When Mr. Silva realized that he needed to establish a business to propagate his findings, he called on his son Joe to help manage the new business, something Joe continues to do today. Then, when Mr. Silva started the new Silva UltraMind Systems business twenty-five years later, at the age of eighty-four, he put Joe in charge.

"When I first came to work for Silva Mind Control International Inc., in 1981," Ed Bernd Jr. recalled, "Joe was among the first to welcome me. 'Around here,' he told me, 'we don't think of you as an employee—we treat you like family.'"

Katherine Sandusky came to work for José Silva in 1990, shortly after graduating from high school. She learned the business—and how to use the Silva techniques in her business and personal life.

She became the first member of her family to earn a college degree, and she started her own Silva business, Avlis Productions Inc., which soon grew into a full-time business with representatives in many countries around the world. (By the way, if you are wondering where the name Avlis came from, just spell it backwards.)

In addition to managing the business, Katherine presents the Silva UltraMind ESP System in the United States and Internationally, and she mentors Silva students. She is also a full-time mother to her young daughter, Lily.

Ed Bernd Jr. grew up in the newspaper business. His motto was "Don't believe anything that you hear and only half of what you see." To say that he was cynical about the reality of ESP would be an understatement. "When I actually *experienced* it for myself, and could produce ESP repeatedly, then I couldn't deny it anymore," he said. "When I realized how valuable this ability is for individuals and how much better life would be on this planet if everybody could use their intuition to get whatever they need without taking from anybody else, without hurting anyone, then I had to get involved. When we reach that point, there will be no more need for crime, no more wars, and life will be good for everyone."

In 1977 Ed attended Instructor Training to learn more, then began teaching the course, and eventually was offered at job at José Silva's Laredo headquarters. "I couldn't pass up an opportunity like that," he said, "and I have been here ever since."

Part One

How to Use More of Your Brain and Mind

1

Brain Power Begins at Alpha

My increasing mental faculties are for serving humanity better.
—JOSÉ SILVA

Have you ever wondered why some people seem to have a magic touch? They always seem to know the right thing to say, they make good decisions, do the right thing, and seem to move easily from one success to the next.

They are not smarter than other people, they don't work any harder than you do, but they are among the 10 percent of people who use more of their brain and mind than everybody else.

They use two areas of their brain, and two dimensions of mind to think with. Imagine what an advantage that is.

Nine out of ten people are able to think with only the beta part of their brain. Approximately one person in ten is able to think with the alpha part of their brain, and then act at the beta level.

In this chapter you are going to learn how to use two parts of your brain and two dimensions of mind consciously, the same way that ultrasuccessful people do.

Imagine how it would be if most people thought that they could only use one leg. If everybody else hopped around on one leg, while you used two legs, you could get around much faster and more easily than they could. That's what it's like when you use "two brains" instead of just one. That's why some people—the ultrasuccessful people—seem to have so much more ability than the average person.

When you learn how to use the alpha part of your brain to think with and then take action at the beta level, you will be using more of your brain and mind than the average person and you will have the ability to achieve great success also.

You will be able to use the subconscious consciously to remove impediments and overcome negative past programming and achieve even greater success in everything that you do from now on.

Millions of people in 103 countries around the world have already benefited from José Silva's pioneering research, and now you will too.

Research on the effectiveness of the Silva techniques has proven that no matter how much—or how little—success you've had up until now, you will benefit.

Single mothers on welfare benefited. So did executives at RCA Records. And adolescent inner city students. And alcoholics. And regular people like you and me.

But the main question is: what does it take for you to be successful with José

Silva's System, and in life?

First, you have to want it. You have to want to be successful. So let's talk about your reasons for reading this book.

Maybe your reasons are personal—for yourself. Maybe you want to help your family. Maybe you want to advance your career. Maybe you want to improve your health and your recreational activities. Whatever your reason is, think about these three questions:

- What do you want?
- How will it help you?
- Why is that important to you?

To increase your desire, think of all the benefits you will derive. Who else will benefit? The more people who will benefit, the more desire you will have to push you towards success.

José Silva says that we are not here just to live it up; we are not here for a seventy-year coffee break. We have a purpose, and that purpose is to solve problems, relieve suffering, and improve living conditions on the planet for ourselves and everyone else, so that when we move on, we will have left behind a better world for those who follow.

Your obligation is to be the best that you can be: the best parent, the best spouse, the best brother or sister, the best employee or employer, because when you are, you will be a better problem solver, and more people will benefit.

The more people who benefit—even complete strangers—the more desire you will have to carry you towards the success that you know, deep within yourself, that you are capable of.

It is important to focus on your reasons for learning this system, and to increase your desire.

Because then, with every technique, you will be thinking about how it can help you to correct problems and make the world a better place to live.

Focusing on your reasons for learning this system is important for another reason too:

When you learn to enter deep levels of mind, which you will begin to do in this chapter—when you go deep within yourself—you will be carrying that desire there with you, and that desire, at those deep inner levels, will produce results.

Whenever you talk with people, that deep inner desire to help them will express itself, and people in your presence will sense it. It will go far beyond the words you use and your body language, and will include the energy that radiates out from your body. That energy is called an *aura*, and in chapter 12 you will learn specific techniques to project your aura and use it to influence people in your presence.

The Importance of the Alpha Level

All of our techniques are designed to function at the alpha level. That is why it is so important to practice the Silva Centering Exercise from time to time to maintain a good deep alpha level. You need to practice it enough in the beginning so that you can relax physically and mentally and remain relaxed while you do your programming. Practice the Silva Centering Exercise at least three times. Mr. Silva recommended accumulating ten hours of practice with the Silva Centering Exercise to ensure that you have established a deep, healthy level of mind to function from.

There are many benefits to being able to use the subconscious consciously. In fact, José Silva said this was his greatest discovery:

a way to use the subconscious consciously, thus converting it to an *inner conscious level.*

What Is the Alpha Level?

Your brain operates on a small amount of electricity, just like a computer. It can process and store information, retrieve that information, and use it to make decisions and solve problems.

Unlike a computer, however, the brain generates and functions with electricity that does not remain at a fixed frequency. Sometimes the brain's electric current vibrates rapidly—twenty times per second or more. Other times it vibrates very slowly, one time per second or less. Scientists call these vibrations *cycles*, or *Hertz*, and have divided the brain frequency spectrum into four different segments, based on the number of cycles per second (cps):

1. Beta, more than 14 cps (typically 20 cps), occurs when your body and mind are active and you focus your eyes.
2. Alpha, 7 to 14 cps, is associated with light sleep and dreaming.
3. Theta, from 4 to 7 cps, is associated with deeper sleep and with the use of hypnosis for such things as painless surgery.
4. Delta, below 4 cps, is associated with deepest sleep.

José Silva reasoned that the best range to use for mental activity would be the range that has the least impedance and the most energy. Of the four frequencies, the alpha frequency has the strongest current and is the most rhythmic. That's why it was the first to be discovered by scientists in the 1920s using the electroenceph-alograph. They named it the *alpha state* after the first letter in the Greek alphabet.

José Silva reasoned that if it was possible to actively use one's mind to analyze problems and come up with solutions while in the alpha state, it seemed logical that this state would be the ideal one in which to think. Why would the alpha level be ideal?

1. It would allow one to think more clearly because of its extra energy.
2. It would enable one to maintain concentration better.
3. Alpha is in the absolute center of the brain's normal operating range, so it would allow access to more information more easily.

But there was a catch. Research revealed that most people do their thinking at the beta frequency! José's research led him to discover that only 10 percent of the population are natural alpha thinkers. It turned out that he himself was one of them.

Most people are using the weakest, least stable frequency to do their thinking: the beta level. Most people, when their brain frequency slows to alpha, enter the subconscious state, then fall asleep. But the superstars stay awake at the alpha level, and do their thinking at alpha.

The alpha level can help you keep you healthy. Entering the alpha level for fifteen minutes once a day will strengthen your immune mechanism and help to keep you healthy. At the alpha level you can learn to overcome all kinds of problems, such as insomnia, tension, migraine headaches, bad habits, and much more.

And you can program to achieve what you want to achieve, and make your dreams come true.

Here is some information that José Silva presented in classes about the alpha level:

The Centering Exercise has to be done to find those deep dimensions where all of these things work. With no deepening, this would never work. It has to be programmed at deep levels for it to work. You have to have that to establish a foundation, to make it work, to make everything work. It is the standard—the proper depth to make it work.

You cannot learn to do it simply by reading about it. You have to take action, to do it, in order to learn to enter the alpha dimension. This is where the Silva Centering Exercise comes in. That has to work before you can make the techniques work.

Every time you practice, you will enter a level deeper than the prior one. We keep doing that until we reach the ideal level, where everything works.

Once you do that, you can activate your mind there, and you've got it made. You can program yourself with the formulas we provide to you so that you can solve any kind of problem.

From there on, when you need to solve a problem, you go to 10 cycles alpha automatically.

You have to get to the right dimension to accomplish all of the things that can be done there.

When you practice the Silva Centering Exercise, you do not need to remain in a fixed position of your body, as you do in yoga. Any position that you feel comfortable in is good enough. You can cross your legs, or uncross them. You can scratch yourself. Cough. Whatever. Just don't open your eyes.

Now if you feel forced to open your eyes, because you feel uncomfortable keeping them closed, then don't force yourself—open your eyes. No problem.

But usually when you open your eyes, you break the level that you are going into, and you have to start over again. But regardless, if you have to open your eyes, then go ahead and do so. Then start over again at the beginning of the exercise.

We are going to give you four ways to learn our System without attending a class:

- Use daily countdown deepening exercises.
- Memorize the Silva Centering Exercise.
- Record the Silva Centering Exercise and play it back to yourself.
- Have someone read the Silva Centering Exercise to you. You can team up with a partner and help each other learn.

If you use a recording of the Silva Centering Exercise, please be sure to use one with José Silva's original wording—his original phrases—not one of the modified versions that were changed by somebody else after his passing. The original Silva Basic Lecture Series and his UltraMind ESP System will have the original version.

Relaxation Leads to Alpha

The Silva System is not "book learning." It is subjective experiencing. It is just like learning any other skill: you must practice to develop expertise and gain the confidence that will let you excel.

When you become passive and relaxed physically and mentally, your brain frequency slows down. This happens when you go to sleep at night. It happens when you are relaxed and daydreaming. But if you haven't learned to stay at alpha when you activate your mind, then your brain frequency will increase whenever you become mentally or physically active.

After you learn to enter the alpha level, then you can learn to activate your mind and remain at the alpha level by practicing a series of "mental calisthenics" that José Silva developed during his twenty-two years of scientific research. He was the first scientist to discover how to do this, and his groundbreaking research was published in the medical journal *Neuropsychology* in 1972.

The fastest and easiest way to learn is to have someone guide you to relax, and then to practice the mental calisthenics. There are several ways to do this without attending a live seminar:

You can go to the web site www.SilvaNow.com and stream or download a recording of the Silva Centering Exercise.

You can also be your own instructor by recording the Silva Centering Exercises and the other conditioning cycles.

You can talk to a recorder as if it were you. You can give yourself instructions to close your eyes and take a deep breath. You can instruct yourself to relax all the parts of your body. You can tell yourself to picture tranquil and passive scenes to induce a relaxed mind.

To get started now, there is a complete script of the Silva Centering Exercise in appendix A in the back of this book. You can follow the instructions and make your own recording, in your own voice. Or you can ask someone else to record it for you.

If you are learning the Silva System along with someone else, you can take turns reading it to each other. The other person can watch you and pace themselves depending on how quickly you relax, and you can do the same for them.

If none of those approaches are practical for you, then you can go to appendix A and follow the instructions there in order to memorize the basic steps that we use in the Silva Centering Exercise, then close your eyes and do it for yourself. José Silva's brother Juan always believed that it is better to do it yourself than to have somebody else guiding you.

If you find yourself making an effort to recall the instructions, and therefore are not relaxing completely, then you can use the Morning Countdown system in appendix B.

José Silva recommended that when you learn on your own, you should accumulate a total of ten hours of practice with the Silva Centering Exercise in order to be confident of your ability to function at the alpha level.

All of our techniques are designed to work at the alpha level. However, once you learn, you will not need to go through the Centering Exercise to get to alpha. The more you practice, the easier it will be to do it. Once you learn the exercise, the sequence, and what to do and how to do it, then practice on your own, without a recording or another person to guide you. If somebody else takes you to the alpha level, then, while you are listening to them, you might not be totally involved. When you have enough desire to do it yourself, you will receive great benefits. If you have that desire, then use it.

When you achieve the state of deep relaxation, physically and mentally, you can be assured that you are at a very deep level of mind.

Tips

After you have completed the training, then you can maintain your ability by using what you have learned to solve problems. We recommend that you go to the alpha level at least once a day, for five minutes. Twice a day is better, three times a day is excellent.

To practice for five minutes each time is good, ten minutes is better, fifteen minutes is excellent.

Now when you are ready to begin, choose the method that is best for you and either use the recording on the www.SilvaNow .com website, or go to Appendix A or B, and follow the instructions.

Positive Thinking and Speaking

Positive thoughts bring me benefits and advantages I desire.

—José Silva

Words have meanings, and the more times we hear them—or think them—the more likely they are to influence us. It is what some people call a "self-fulfilling prophecy." The words and thoughts make impressions on our brain neurons, and when they have been impressed on enough brain neurons, those ideas become part of our reality.

This can help us or hurt us. A Silva graduate named Steve Sellers, a radio announcer at a radio station in San Antonio, Texas, demonstrated how powerful our words can be. "We project a positive image to our listeners by eliminating the negatives," Sellers explained. "Other stations' meteorologists announce a partly cloudy day—on our station that same day is partly sunny."

Within thirty days of starting this approach, the station, which for years had been the overlooked stepchild in the broadcasting chain, turned into a viable force in the San Antonio radio market.

Hector Chacon, a high-school basketball coach in Laredo, Texas, found that one simple change in the way he coached his players turned a losing season around.

"When we stop focusing on the end result that we desire, and start thinking instead about mistakes, we are likely to make more mistakes," he explained.

That's what he was doing. His team would build up a lead in the first half. At halftime he would focus on the errors in an attempt to correct them. He'd confront the players with their mistakes and challenge them to correct them. All the mental pictures were negative—pictures of the problem. They would blow the lead and lose the game.

After the first five conference games, they were 1–4.

Then the coach changed his way of talking to his players. "I called on a friend of mine who had learned the Silva System, and asked if he had any ideas that could help me," Coach Chacon said. "He spent twenty minutes on the phone with me, explaining the principles of positive thinking." He followed the advice.

"In that night's game, I still pointed out the mistakes," he said, "but after that, I made sure that I told the players exactly what I wanted them to do. And I took it one step further. I reminded each player of a successful play he had made, and told them to do it like that again."

The results? The first time out with this simple technique, they beat a team that had beaten them a few weeks earlier. They beat them by a score of 80 to 47! In their final nine conference games, after that one simple change in Coach Chacon's approach, they had an 8–1 record.

How Words Can Hurt You

Can your words really hurt you? A fifty-five-year-old man who attended the Silva training in Albuquerque, New Mexico, had a perfect example of how this happens after reflecting on his language for a while: "For years I've used the phrases, 'I can't see that,' 'It's a pain in the neck,' and 'It's a pain in the . . .' Well, I won't finish the phrase, but let me explain: I wear glasses, I have headaches in the back of my head, and I have hemorrhoids!"

That got a laugh from the other members of the seminar, but when a person has suffered with those problems for several decades, it is no joke.

Here is what to do when you notice that you are using negative words and phrases:

Stop, and cancel out the negative words by saying, "Cancel-cancel." Then replace the negative words with positive words.

A Secret Way to Protect Yourself from Negativity

Sometimes you might find yourself in a situation where you cannot say "Cancel-cancel." For instance, what do you do if your sales manager or a customer says something negative to you? If you tell them "Cancel-cancel" they might just cancel-cancel you!

Instead of that, just give them a big zero. In a computer, the program uses either a zero or a one—that is, the circuit is either open or closed. When it is open, nothing gets through.

So give the negative words a big zero by saying, "Oh." For example: "You really fouled up this time!" "Oh? Well, what can I do to make it right?" By doing that, you are canceling out the negative thought, and replacing it with a positive thought.

These techniques work. Read what a big New Jersey pharmaceutical manufacturing firm had to say after learning the Silva techniques:

"'Cancel-cancel' and 'better and better' are new phrases being spoken at our company after 150 employees participated in the Silva training.

"For over 150 employees, the phrase 'better and better' is synonymous with a new way of thinking, a philosophy of one's own inner consciousness and a different attitude about life, work, and other people."

A company merchandising director said, "Even though I went into the course with a certain amount of 'show me' attitude, I have to admit that I thoroughly enjoyed the program. It gave me a new sense of awareness about myself and the importance of working with fellow employees," he continued. "I am applying what I learned by trying to develop the ability to channel my interests and accomplishments so there is less wasted time and motion. The concept certainly makes you stop and think."

Be Kind to Yourself

It takes time to learn any new skill. And positive thinking is a new skill. We have been programmed, biologically and by our parents and teachers, to watch out for trouble. This helps us to survive in the physical world, because there are many things in the world that have the potential to harm us.

Therefore you might notice that you are using quite a few negative words during the day.

Some people become depressed when they discover this. They beat themselves up mentally and verbally: "Wow, am I negative! I can't even pass the first part of this course!"

We'd suggest a different approach.

Instead of looking at the downside—how many negative things you might be saying—look at the good side. Or as somebody once put it, "Look for the good and praise it."

Now what, you might ask, can be good about realizing that you are saying so many negative things?

The fact that you noticed it is good. Now that you are aware, you can take steps to change.

Once you begin to think and talk about the things you want rather than the things you don't want, you have opened a big door to success.

Evaluate Your Progress

You might be surprised just how much this one simple exercise—Mental Housecleaning—can help you. To get an idea of how much this can benefit you, do this:

Notice during the day how people respond to you as you use positive words and phrases instead of negative ones.

At night, when you are ready to go to sleep, notice whether you feel better than you normally do, and if you go to sleep easier and faster than before.

In the morning, when it is time to get up, notice whether you find it a little easier to get up and face the new day with its challenges and opportunities.

Prosperity Programming

From time to time people ask us to include statements about prosperity and abundance in the Silva conditioning cycles.

They see the various "prosperity" books and tapes and courses on the market, with affirmations like, "I love money," "Money is attracted to me like a magnet," "I deserve to be prosperous," and so forth. Why don't we add affirmations like that to the Silva conditioning cycles? they ask us.

People also ask us to add affirmations about self-esteem and self-confidence. They suggest affirmations such as, "I love myself," "I am worthy of love," "I am capable of handling any situation," and on and on.

There are two reasons why José Silva chose not to include statements like this:

First, they don't work. In fact, statements like these usually do more harm than good.

Second, the Silva Centering Exercise already includes statements that, when followed, will make you prosperous and confident and give you everything you need in life, and more.

Formula for Success

José Silva included a formula for success in the Silva Centering Exercise. This formula is included in every Silva course, and in many of our audio recordings. It is a simple formula, deceptively simple. In fact, many people overlook it and never realize how powerful it is.

The formula is found just before the Centering Exercise ends. This is the most powerful point in the exercise. That gives you an idea of how important José Silva feels it is.

Here is the formula: *You will continue to strive to take part in con-structive and creative activities to make this a better world to live in, so that when we move on we shall have left behind a better world for those who follow. You will consider the whole of humanity, depending on their ages, as fathers or mothers, brothers or sisters, sons or daughters. You are a superior human being. You have greater understanding, compassion, and patience with others.*

Why It Works

Let's take a look at each element of this formula to see why he included it, and why the formula works:

You will continue to strive . . . It is important that you make a sincere attempt to do what you were sent here to do. We each have different talents and different levels of ability. As long as you are doing what you are capable of doing, this is what counts. Others may get greater results than you do, but as long as you are doing as much as you can, you are fulfilling your purpose.

. . . to take part in constructive and creative activities . . . How do you know you are doing what you were sent here to do? This is the measure. We are made in the image of the Creator. This means that we should create, not destroy. We should construct, not tear down.

. . . to make this a better world to live . . . This is the tangible mea-sure of our success. We should always improve conditions on the planet. That which hurts or destroys is wrong; it means that you are going in the wrong direction. When your efforts solve prob-lems and make things better, you are going in the right direction.

. . . so that when we move on we shall have left behind a better world for those who follow. Why would you want to do that? Why improve conditions for others, rather than for yourself?

This is a statement of unselfishness, of doing something for someone who cannot possibly compensate or repay you in any way. Prosperity does not come through a barter system. When you are doing what you were sent here to do, you will receive everything that you need to help and encourage you continue to do your job. This is a good topic to meditate on, to reflect on at level. (When we say "level," we mean at the alpha level.)

When José Silva was asked about this statement, if the intent was to signify the unselfish attitude that is required, he answered, "If we had not had that attitude, we wouldn't have the Silva System today."

José Silva's own life offers many examples of his unselfish attitude. He helped all who asked, and never accepted any compensation. After he had developed his System, he offered it to the U.S. government free of charge. He was simply doing his job.

You will consider the whole of humanity, depending on their ages, as fathers or mothers, brothers or sisters, sons or daughters. José Silva points out that animals protect their own kin, but not others. God, on the other hand, treats all people equally.

We were made in the image of God, and given a task to do. We were given the ability to take part in constructive and creative activities, just as God does. We were assigned here to be helpers.

If we are to help God, we must help God's creatures. Most people have a natural tendency to help their own kin. We can expand that to help everyone.

But notice that the relationships we have with our family members vary, according to the specific relationship:

We show a special respect to our parents. They brought us into this world, they cared for us when we were helpless, guided us the best they knew how.

We grew up with our brothers and sisters, shared everything with them, including experiences and memories. No matter how much we fought with them, we always had unconditional love for them, and were always ready to come to their aid or defense.

Our children depend on us. We nurture and guide them. We protect them. We shelter them when necessary, and encourage them to go out into the world when it is time for that.

Many people talk about loving humanity, our global family. But notice that we don't love each member of our family the same way. We have different feelings, special feelings, for each, depending on our relationship with them.

José Silva expanded the meaning of loving humanity:

- When you interact with people older than you, old enough to be your parents, do you show them the respect that parents deserve? Do you treat them way you would your own parents?

- When you interact with people your own age, do you have the unconditional love that you have for a brother or sister, that allows you to say, "I may not like what you are doing, but I love you because I recognize that we both come from the same source and that source is good"?

- Are you willing to help those who are younger than you, the same way you would help your own children? The next time you are involved with a younger person, ask yourself if you are saying to them what you would say to your own child, if you are doing for them what you would do for your own child. This is what is meant by loving humanity. This is Godlike behavior.

You are a superior human being. We are the most highly evolved life form on the planet. With that superior position comes special responsibility. Does being superior mean that we can exploit whatever we find here on the planet, and use it for our own selfish purposes? Or should we imitate the Creator, and nurture and protect what we have been given to use? Once you have learned how to center yourself, how to communicate subjectively, how to get help from the other side so that you can do God's will, you have talents and abilities that are superior to those who have not yet done this.

You have greater understanding, compassion, and patience with others. Because you are able to enter deep levels of mind and view things from a higher perspective, you have a better understanding of what your task is.

From this higher (superior) perspective, you are closer to God. You have a desire to correct problems and help all of God's creation and all of God's creatures to be more productive and successful and happy.

You do not get this perspective from the beta level. From the physical level, it seems that when somebody else gets something, then you can't have it. From a higher level, you see that the more you give, the more you receive.

This is not something that we can intellectualize, but something that we must live.

You also understand that not everyone has developed this kind of understanding yet, and you are patient with them as you help your fathers and mothers, brothers and sisters, sons and daughters to express their Godlike nature, just as you have done.

Creating a Paradise

Perhaps it is a big order to live up to all of that. Maybe only a saint can really do it. But those who come the closest are the ones who have the greatest prosperity.

They feel good about themselves, because they are more Godlike, and are closer to God. They have great self-confidence, because they have a sure sense of purpose that conforms to the reason they were assigned to this planet.

This is not something that you develop at beta, or at light levels of alpha.

When you enter deep levels, you will develop a real understanding and appreciation for these statements.

But for them to make a difference in your life, you have to turn them into action.

The more active you are, the more Godlike you are.

José Silva had the deep understanding that few people have had. And he was always extremely energetic and active.

This is a combination that has made him world-famous, that has put the Silva System into more than one hundred countries, and has helped millions of people worldwide to change their lives for the better.

Even in his eighties, José Silva continued to be active, to travel the world, to spread the message and teach his System.

He did not do this to accumulate great wealth. He lived in the same modest house in Laredo for fifty years. He had no investments other than his own business. He put most of the money he earned back into the business, in order to reach more and more of the people he considered his fathers and mothers, brothers and sisters, sons and daughters.

If you appreciate the benefits that you have received from his System, then it is time now for you to take steps to carry on the most important part of José Silva's work:

Make this formula a part of your life. Meditate on it. Put it into action. Review it daily at your center until it is as natural to you as breathing.

Help make José Silva's dream a reality: to convert the planet into a paradise.

The Three Faces of You

Repeating so-called "affirmations" in an attempt to overcome problems and shortcomings can actually do more harm than good.

We think that we believe certain things. And we actually do believe certain things. But often these two are not the same.

This truth is illustrated by a story about a tightrope walker who walked across a wire that was strung across Niagara Falls. As he walked, he pushed a loaded wheelbarrow in front of him. Being a good entertainer, the tightrope walker put on a good show by acting as if he were going to fall, but catching his balance at the last moment.

Finally he got to the other side as the crowd applauded thunderously. He acknowledged the cheering crowd and took his bows.

Then he approached a man in the crowd and asked if he thought that the tightrope walker could cross the falls safely again back to the other side.

"Sure you could," the man answered. "Are you certain?" the tightrope walker asked.

"Absolutely," the spectator answered. "You are the greatest tightrope walker in the world. I'm sure you can make it back across!"

"OK," the tightrope walker said, "since you are so sure, get in the wheelbarrow, and let's go!"

Resolving the Conflict

Often we think that we know what we want and what we believe, only to find that "it ain't necessarily so."

Dr. J. Wilfred Hahn, longtime consultant and researcher for José Silva, developed a model to help us understand how we function.

He said that we are really like three people. He identified these as Wilfred, Willie, and Will.

Wilfred is the scientist, the logical, beta-oriented part of each one of us, who has to have explanations for everything, to make sure that everything seems logical.

Willie is the voice within, the alpha part of us, the part that deals with feelings and core beliefs and old programming, the part that manages the body. Wilfred and Willie are often in conflict with each other. No matter how much Wilfred may understand something, you also have to get the message through to Willie.

To get back to our discussion of affirmations, it may sound perfectly logical to Wilfred to make a statement at the beta level about how much you believe you deserve to be wealthy. But how does Willie interpret this statement?

Willie is not going to get into the wheelbarrow. Willie is going to say, "If you believe that you deserve money, why do you need to use affirmations?"

A reflex action will take place. Instead of convincing Willie that you really do deserve money, you will reinforce just the opposite thought. Willie will feel that you do not believe that you deserve money.

So how do we resolve the conflict between Wilfred and Willie? According to Dr. Hahn, that takes "an act of Will."

Create a Picture-Perfect World

When we forget to use visualization and imagination,
it is like not using our minds.

—JOSÉ SILVA

The language of the brain, the language of the mind and the subjective dimension, is not English or Spanish or German—it is visual.

Everybody understands pictures. Your brain understands pictures. It may not understand every language in the world, but it does understand pictures. Your mind understands pictures.

When you have a problem and you want to correct it mentally, you need to transfer it from the objective dimension—the physical dimension—to the subjective—the mental—dimension.

You also need to use the correct language. Let's learn how.

The Universal Language

Children learn best by observing, by watching to see what people do. Even if they don't understand what you are telling them, they know what they see.

In the physical world it can be difficult to work with somebody and to help them if you don't speak the same language. Mentally that is not a problem, because the language of the mind is visual, and everybody "gets the picture," so to speak.

The Mental Screen, which we will learn about next, is a communications tool.

The Mental Screen allows you to transfer problems from the objective dimension to the subjective dimension so that you can correct them.

The Mental Screen is also the means by which you can communicate in the subjective dimension:

- You can communicate with your own body, and your own inner conscious level.
- You can communicate with other people, with their minds and their brains and their bodies.
- You can communicate in this manner with higher intelligence, with our helpers on the other side.
- You can get information in this manner—with the use of your Mental Screen—from wherever that information exists.

Two Different Worlds

The objective world of the body and the subjective world of the mind are two different things, so before we go any further, let's define some terms:

- First, the word *see*. You *see* with your eyes. That is the only way to see anything—with your eyes. Whenever you focus your eyes or attempt to focus your eyes, your brain goes to 20 cycles per second. You can use any of your other senses at alpha, but the sense of sight requires your brain to be at beta.
- Next, the word *visualize*. You visualize with your mind. To visualize means that you remember what something looks like. In order to remember, that means that you have to have seen it, or imagined it, before. Visualization is not like seeing. It is not even like dreaming. It is like remembering. Visualization is memory, the memory of what something looks like. You do not use your eyes to visualize; you use your mind.
- Next, the word *imagine*. To imagine means to think about what something looks like that you have never experienced before—something you have not seen before, or for that matter imagined before. Because you have not seen this thing before, imagining it is a creative process.

Let's take an example that uses seeing, visualization, and imagination.

Do you remember seeing the dog Lassie on television or in a movie? If not, then recall any dog that you have seen. Do you remember what the dog looked like?

- What size is this dog?
- How big?
- How long was the hair?
- What color was it?
- What did its tail look like?
- Its ears?

Remembering what you have seen before is *visualization.* And you have just visualized a dog that you have seen previously.

How many legs did the dog have? Four? Now, can you imagine what the dog would look like if it had six legs? Where would the other two legs be? At the front? The back? In the middle? Where would they be? Imagine what that would look like.

Now you have just used *imagination* to create a mental picture of something that you have never seen or imagined before.

It is very simple. You can do it with your eyes open, or closed. You can do it at beta or at alpha.

In order to imagine things and have them manifest in the physical world, your visualization and imagination must be at alpha.

For now, it is easiest for you to do this with your eyes closed, because you shut out distractions. Later, with practice, you can learn how to function at alpha with your eyes open and unfocused.

Now, if you go back and recall the dog with six legs that you imagined—and recall what the dog looks like, and where the two extra legs are—the front, the back, the middle—then you are visualizing, because you are recalling what something looks like that you imagined previously.

A few people have very vivid mental images when they do this. Most people have some kind of mental image. Some of us simply know what the dog would look like. These people might say that they imagine what the mental image would look like.

The good news is—that's all that is required to be successful in your functioning in the subjective dimension.

You want to get accustomed to thinking about what things look like. Some people use words to think things through; others use feelings. These are all good, and are important. It is also important, especially for mental functioning—in the subjective dimension—that you think visually as well.

This is very important when you use a programming technique like the Three-Scenes Technique, which you will learn in the next chapter. It is important because you must first visualize the problem that you need to correct, and then you imagine the problem corrected. You use imagination to create the end result that you want to manifest in the physical world.

Would you like a technique to help you develop and improve your ability to visualize and imagine on your Mental Screen? We have a technique to do that. As an added bonus, this same technique will also help to improve your memory. You receive two benefits for the price of one.

First, let's define the Mental Screen, and show you how to locate it.

Your Mental Screen

Your Mental Screen can be like a surround movie screen, or a giant 360-degree computer screen.

Your Mental Screen will be upwards, and about 30 feet away from you. The Mental Screen is about 20 degrees above your horizontal level of sight, like when you are in a theater, and it can be all around you. You can project and detect images on the screen behind you, off to the sides, if you need to.

You want your Mental Screen to be above the horizontal plane of sight. You want to physically turn your eyes up slightly. Not so much that you are uncomfortable, but definitely upwards. This helps to produce more alpha rhythm in the brain. Nobody knows why for sure, but it does. It will help you to stay in alpha while you are using your visualization and imagination to identify problems and create solutions.

To locate your Mental Screen, begin with your eyes closed, turned slightly upward from the horizontal plane of sight, at an angle of approximately 20 degrees.

The area that you perceive with your mind is your Mental Screen.

Without using your eyelids as screens, sense your Mental Screen to be out, away from your body.

To improve the use of your Mental Screen, project images or mental pictures onto the screen, especially images having color. Concentrate on mentally sensing and visualizing true color.

So you do this with your eyes closed, and turned slightly upward, and you imagine the screen to be out and away from you. This is where you are going to project mental imagery, or to detect something, when you visualize on your Mental Screen.

So to transmit something, you project it to your Mental Screen. To detect it, you create a mental image on your Mental Screen.

Improving Visualization, Imagination, Clairvoyance, and Memory

One excellent way to improve the use of your Mental Screen is to learn techniques to improve your memory.

Using visualization, imagination, and association makes it easier to remember things. Whenever you need to remember something, remember what it looks like.

We tend to remember things that we associate with having a good time. Most people can remember great birthday presents they received when they were young, or special events like their first date or their senior prom.

Your brain has the capacity to remember a great deal. Scientists say—and it has become a cliché—that the human brain is the most highly structured and complex object in the universe. You'll be amazed at what it is capable of—at what *you* are capable of.

Our objective is not to give you a memory course. You can do that on your own with any of the excellent books by Harry Lorayne or others who use a system like the Memory Peg system, which relies on visualization and imagination.

How Words Can Help You

Words can often help you to create better mental pictures. You can use words to describe a scene to yourself in order to help you picture it mentally.

For instance, think of a relative or a friend that you know very well, and think of what their face looks like. It might help you to describe to yourself what their hair looks like, their forehead, the color of the skin, their eyes, their nose, cheeks, the character of their face.

If you are visualizing a project that you are working on, it might help you to imagine that you are discussing the project with someone, explaining how to go about doing it. This can help you to create a detailed mental picture of it.

Alpha Break

Here is a special technique that José Silva developed to help you improve your visualization and imagination. You can do this at beta. It is even more effective when you do it at the alpha level.

To help you develop and enhance the faculty of controlled daydreaming, a technique designed to enable you to use your day-dreaming faculties for constructive purposes, recall a pleasant, relaxing daydream, or an event you may have experienced in the past. Make an effort to reexperience the pleasant feelings associated with this dream or event, and all of the visual components. Take your time for this.

Once you have selected the dream or event, modify and change it in as many ways as you can, employing changes in colors, characters, situations, structures, and end results. I will give you time for this.

In succeeding practice sessions, you may choose to employ this daydreaming mechanism in more practical applications, such as programming successful end results.

You may utilize this technique during the day, in your leisure time, with your eyes open, by employing the natural mechanism of a daydream state, which is commonly observed in people who are daydreaming.

To use this mechanism, stare into your environment wherever you desire, defocusing your vision in the process: that is, staring but not focusing your eyesight on anything in particular.

Once you have activated this mechanism, mentally picture your programming objective, in terms of a sequence or series of events, starting by first visualizing the problem, then visualizing or imagining the application of corrective effects, and lastly, by imagining the desired end results—the solution.

Visualization and Imagination

Here are transcripts of recordings we made of José Silva at an Instructor Training session:

Visualization is a previous impression, impressed on your brain or mind.

It is a receiving, detecting mechanism.

We can detect with the left brain hemisphere, we can detect with the right brain hemisphere.

In other words, in order to perceive it with the left hemisphere, it must exist. Whether somebody created something, or it is the sense of sight, then you make an impression on your brain.

The sense of sight works like a camera. It makes a negative and impresses it on your brain, your left brain. And a duplicate is transferred to the right brain.

Receiving information, receiving information, receiving information, is energy. Visualization is the receiver, imagination is the transmitter.

You can also visualize with your right hemisphere. But in this case you can visualize what has been impressed on somebody else's brain.

This is why, if a person is injured a thousand miles away, and you know about that person, and you want to know how seriously hurt she is, or injured, you go to your level, turn on your intercom—your right brain—and the right brain functions on a different band, like FM does, not AM, and you are tuning into his brain and getting information from his brain and transferring it to yours. Then you will know what happened to him. Because everything that has happened to him has been recorded on his brain already.

Now usually all of this becomes a lot easier if the intention is to help the individual to solve his problem. Not just to know. This doesn't go far enough, just to know. Eventually you will not receive anything, if you are just trying to have fun by wanting to know for no purpose whatsoever.

Your purpose is to follow through, to help this individual to correct his problem, solve his problem, keep him from suffering. That's the main purpose.

So we say the brain, the mind—left brain, right brain—were created to detect information that we can consider, that we don't want, and make a correction.

So information, if we cannot perceive it with the left, we can perceive it with the right.

But we must follow through with the intention of helping correct the problem. Because that's all we are here for. We were sent to planet earth to correct problems that cause people to suffer, to make this planet a better place to live. That's it. No other use.

Now we are using it to steal from others, to hurt others, to kill others, and it's wrong, because it is all left brain. If they had developed the right brain, they wouldn't even have attempted it, because they would have become spiritual. They would have become fully developed human beings.

A person who uses only the left brain hemisphere cannot fully evolve into becoming a human being.

Just keep in mind that a human being is not one who looks like one, it is one who acts like one.

To be considered a human being, you must participate—take part—in humanitarian acts. Then you have qualified and passed the test to be considered a human being. If you have not taken part in humanitarian acts, you have not yet been in a position to be considered a human being. You have not been tested, in other words.

Now everybody knows the difference between visualization and imagination?

Keep in mind that we visualize and imagine with the left, and we visualize and imagine with the right. Imagination with the left is fantasy, or rearranging what exists so it will serve a better . . . something, whatever that is. What you are doing is altering what exists, modifying it, to get better results out of it. That is left-brain imagination.

Right-brain imagination is creating something that has never happened, has not occurred yet. That is the beginning of creation, the beginning of inventions, the beginning of discoveries. That happens for the first time. That's right-brain imagination.

Visualization means the same thing: detecting information. One hemisphere detects information in the objective world, and the other—right brain—detects information in the subjective world.

Subjective remembering can be considered spiritual, nonphysical, immaterial, but energetic. In religion it is called *spiritual.*

Why Turn the Eyes Up 20 Degrees?

Why 20 degrees? Because it has been found that when you turn your eyes up 20 degrees relative to your face, you have a stronger production of alpha. Nobody knows why. It is believed that when the eyes were becoming evolved in your body, they were up before they were fully evolved. Then they came down so you could see with them.

We evolved from delta to theta to alpha to beta. So we must have been evolving alpha while the eyes were turned up, before we had a full, complete eye to see with. So finally when we got to beta, it came down to see with. Turned up, it is like going back to alpha again. That has been proven scientifically: Turn eyes up, more alpha. It is like a switch.

So for us it is better to turn them up in order to help us to hold onto alpha.

The problem is, in most cases, not finding alpha, but staying on alpha for a longer period of time. This helps us to lock in on alpha, helps us stay on it, like the Alpha Sound.

Program Yourself for Success

*We don't want to gain at somebody else's loss,
we want to gain while helping the other person to also gain.*

—José Silva

In the introduction we mentioned that we don't solve problems by working on the problems.

That is because we move in the direction of our dominant thoughts.

Everything begins with a thought:

Mind guides brain, and brain guides body.

That doesn't mean that you should pretend that a problem doesn't exist. José Silva advised that in order to solve a problem, you must:

First, be aware that the problem exists.

Then know the correct technique to apply to solve the problem, and how to apply the technique correctly.

José Silva developed a technique to do those things. When you apply the technique correctly, the way he taught us to apply it, then the majority of your thoughts will be about the solution, not the problem.

In fact, we do away with the problem. He said that once you have a plan and you are working your plan, then it isn't a "problem" anymore:

It is a "project."

That is how we go beyond the problem to the solution.

If it is a very big project, so big that it might take some time to accomplish, then concentrate on benchmarks along the way. If the problem is that you can't walk and you want to be able to run a marathon, then concentrate on what you want to do in the next week or two.

Three days from now, if you can walk a little farther than before, that is a great indication that you might be doing the right thing, so keep doing it, and keep looking for more indications of how to proceed.

Advice about Learning New Techniques

Here is something to keep in mind whenever you are learning something new: It is best not to mix systems together. If you use some type of yoga meditation to get to level, for instance, it might not work for you in this context. It might be great for the goals that they have in yoga, but it won't necessarily get you to the precise level that is required for the Silva techniques to work for you.

Three Short Steps to Success

After you learn to enter the alpha level, the most valuable tools you have are visualization and imagination. Use them to solve problems whenever you can, no matter whose problems they are, and no matter whether you receive any benefit for yourself or not.

José Silva's Three-Scenes Technique is a mental technique you can apply at the alpha level to identify and analyze the problem, then go beyond the problem all the way to the solution, the desired end result.

Here is the formula for the Three-Scenes Technique:

The Three-Scenes Technique

Go to your center with the 3 to 1 Method.

The 3 to 1 Method takes advantage of the conditioned responses that you developed in the Silva Centering Exercise. Here is how you do it:

Find a comfortable position, close your eyes, take a deep breath, and mentally repeat and visualize the number 3, three times. You have already associated the number 3 with physical relaxation, so your body will relax when you do this.

Take another deep breath and while exhaling, mentally repeat and visualize the number 2, three times. In the Silva Centering Exercise, you related the number 2 to mental relaxation.

When you relax physically and mentally, your brain frequency will lower to the alpha level.

Take another deep breath, and while exhaling mentally, repeat and visualize the number 1, three times, and you are at level 1, the alpha level, which is at the center of the brain frequency spectrum, and functions at the midbrain area, in the center of your brain. We will call this your *center*.

Once you are at your center, create and project into your Mental Screen, directly in front of you, a scene of the problem. You learned how to locate your Mental Screen in chapter 3.

Recall details of what the problem looks like in this first scene, directly in front of you. Make a good study of the problem so that you are completely aware of all aspects of it.

If you have programmed in this manner previously for this particular project, then take into account any changes that have taken place since your most recent programming session.

After making a good study of the problem, of the existing situation, then shift your awareness to your left, approximately 15 degrees. In a second scene, to the left of the first scene—towards your left—mentally picture yourself taking action and doing something to correct the problem, and imagine the correction beginning to take place.

Now in the third scene, another 15 degrees farther to the left—to your left—create and project an image of the solution.

Imagine many people benefiting from the solution to this problem. The more people who benefit, the better.

Anytime in the future when you think of this project, visualize the image that you created of the solution in the third scene.

Program the Future in the Past

Everything begins with a thought. First you think a thing, then you do it. With the Three-Scenes Technique, we create the solution, in the subjective, nonphysical, world-of-the-mind dimension.

It is completed—in the subjective dimension. The problem has been solved, and we have a solution.

There is no time or space in the subjective dimension. However, in the physical world, we deal with time and space, so it may take longer for the solution to appear in the physical world.

We have a solution in the world of the mind, and will see it soon in the world of the body. Therefore José Silva said that we should "program in the future in a past-tense sense."

When you have your eyes open, at beta, you might see that the problem still exists in the physical world. When that happens—"whenever you happen to think of the project"—immediately recall the image that you created of the solution in the third scene.

The more confident that you are that you have already created the solution and that therefore the solution already exists, the sooner you will see the solution in the physical world.

How do you develop that confidence?

By having successes. Every time you have a success, your belief in the technique and in your apply it to achieve results will increase. We will talk more about faith in chapter 11. Faith is composed of three elements: desire, belief, and expectation, or hope.

The more serious the problem is, the more desire you will have. The more people who will benefit, the more desire you will have.

Belief comes from success, as we just mentioned.

Expectation, or hope, is the solution that you created in the third scene.

Desire pushes you to take action. The more you think about the benefits of the solution, the more desire you have.

Belief gives you confidence and sustains you.

Hope is the target; it keeps you focused on the solution rather than the problem.

Why We Place the Future on the Left

If you are wondering why we go from right to left when moving into the future, Mr. Silva observed that phenomenon in his research, and went on to verify that images (mental images, not physical ones) of the future came from the left, while images of the past came from the right.

During his research, Mr. Silva used to age-regress the research subjects, most of whom were children. He would take them back to an earlier time in their lives, and even do prenatal age regression, whereby he would take them back—mentally—to a time before they were born, to see what kind of stories they would tell him.

He found that he could regress the subjects back hundreds of years, through many different lifetimes. That does not necessarily prove the idea of reincarnation; it only proves that they could detect information.

He began to notice that when he would move the children back and forward in time very rapidly, they would lean to one side or the other. For instance, he might get them to level (he used hypnosis back then) and ask them to go back one hundred years, then two hundred years, then three hundred years. When he did this, they would lean to the side. So he asked them why.

They said that the pictures—the mental images—were moving by very rapidly. It was as if they were sitting on a bus, and it would accelerate so fast that it would cause their body to lean to the side. They said that the images of the past would come from the right, and the images of the future from the left.

Being a curious scientist, Mr. Silva wanted a theory to explain this. It seemed to him that we were getting out of the physical dimension and into the spiritual dimension.

He decided that if the earth (representing the physical dimension) was spinning toward the east, then the future would be to the east. So he tried facing east while at his level, but that didn't work.

He could not move around in time the way he wanted to. Here is the way he explained it:

Imagine you are looking at the earth. The north pole is to the top, the south pole to the bottom. The earth is turning towards the east, which means that it is turning to the right.

Now let us do this: Let us imagine that the physical dimension is a train that is going from left to right (towards the east). Let me see if I can draw a picture of this train for you. Imagine that you are looking at it from above.

>>>>>>>>>>>>>>>>>>>>>>>>>>

Now if you get off the train to the left side—the north side of the train—and you look to the "future"—that is, you look in the direction that the train is going in, you will not see where the train is going. Let me draw a picture of a person who has gotten off the train and is looking in the direction that the train is going:

In order to see the train, so that you can see where it is going, and where it has been, you have to turn 90 degrees and face south, *towards* the train:

Now if you, the subject (↓), look to the left, you can see where the train is going; if you look to the right, you can see where the train has been. I am talking about the subject looking to his/her left or right. Something like this:

Towards the future

Towards the past

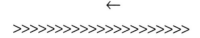

Suppose you decide you want to get off the other side of the train, the side towards the south?

You cannot get off that side, because there are no doors over there.

If you will think about it, or if you will get a piece of paper and draw a globe, you can see how this works:

If the earth represents the physical dimension, and you exit the earth towards the north—go out over the north pole—into the subjective dimension—and you turn and look back towards the earth, then the earth is turning towards your left, to the future. If you look to your right, you will see where it has been, the past.

It does not matter where we are facing physically. This applies to the subjective—mental—dimension, and when you use the Three-Scenes Technique, it works automatically.

In the physical dimension, Mr. Silva explained, the past is behind us, the present is our present position, and the future is in front of us.

In the subjective (mental) dimension, the past is to your right, the present is in front of you, and the future is to your left.

That is why, in the Three-Scenes Technique, we visualize the problem—the existing situation—in front of us, and imagine and visualize the solution in an image to our left.

Programming for Other People

There are many other ways to use the Three-Scenes Technique.

You can use it for self-programming, to help you perform better, as well as for better health and well-being.

Once you have developed and tested your ESP, which you can do in our book *Silva UltraMind Systems ESP for Business Success*, published by G&D Media, you can use the Three-Scenes Technique to program for other people in order to help them overcome problems and accomplish their tasks.

You can use the Three-Scenes Technique to program a glass of water so that it can be used for healing, or for other purposes. Get an ordinary water glass, fill it with water, and hold it with the fingers of both hands. Spread your fingers apart, and do not let the fingers of your right hand touch the fingers of your left hand. Energy from your right hand will flow through the water and be collected by the palm of your left hand. Enter your level and use the Three-Scenes Technique to program for whatever you need.

Graduates have reported that they have programmed water to help loved ones to stop drinking, lose weight, and reach other important goals.

Silva graduates who were far away from a sick relative report that they programmed a get-well card and mailed it to their loved ones.

Businesspeople tell us that they program objects to help them make sales and better negotiations.

You can learn to do all these things and even more when you develop your ability to project your mind and use your ESP, as you can learn in *Silva UltraMind ESP System for Business Success.*

Some Programming Tips

When we say to "make a good study of the problem," this means we should observe the details.

Once you program to correct the problem, you do not go back to the problem image. Whenever you think of the problem—which we will call a "project" from now on—immediately visualize the solution image you have created in the third scene.

When you program, look for objective feedback—something in the physical world that you can see with your eyes—to let you know what effect your programming is having. We recommend that you program in such a way that you would expect something to happen within the next few days.

If you see improvement, then you know to keep on programming the way you have been doing. If the situation gets worse, then go to your center and analyze what happened. You might realize that you should alter your programming.

If there isn't any change after three days, then try anything you can think of to see if you can start making progress. Sometimes you need to program more; sometimes you need to program less.

The more desire you have, the better. How many reasons do you have for wanting to achieve this goal, or correct this problem? Perhaps there are five benefits that you can think of. Go to your center and think about it again; you might come up with five more benefits. Then you will have twice as much motivation.

"The bigger your project is," José Silva told us, "the more help you will get from higher intelligence. What I mean by bigger," he explained, "is how many people will benefit. If you are just programming something for yourself only, then you are on your own; you are not going to get any help. But if your programming will benefit many people, then you will get help. The more people who will benefit, the more help you will get."

Guidance from José Silva

Here is some more advice from José Silva, based on his fifty-five years of research and experience in this field:

> Keep your programming in the possibility area. This does not mean to limit yourself, but if you program for something that you don't believe, deep inside, that you can achieve, there is little chance that you will achieve it, at least not any time soon.
>
> Remember that we do not control other people. If somebody wants to drink and get drunk, they are going to drink and get drunk. If a person wants to be with somebody else, it is a waste of time to program for that person to be with you. You can program that a person will have a desire to change—to stop drinking, for instance. Once the person desires it enough, they will take the necessary steps to bring it about.
>
> Regarding setting time limits: If we could prophesy 100 percent, we could do that. But nobody can prophesy 100 percent.

Get the problem resolved regardless of when it happens.

We cannot obligate or force the intelligence that's guiding us to do what we think we should do. It does it the way it thinks it should.

If you are asking for money—for instance, "Please let me win the lottery"—let the money come any way it needs to come. Higher intelligence knows how to get it to you. Don't be specific, or program that it should come to you in a specific way. Let it come any way, as long as you get it. That's what counts.

We can't boss higher intelligence around, to do it the way we think, at the time we want it. Higher intelligence will do it when it is the best thing to do, at the right time. We don't know about that. We may think we do. It is a step forward, and a step backwards. That's part of it.

On your way towards your goal, if you find a problem, and you solve the problem, it places you on the path towards your goal.

But if, after this, you come across another problem, and if this second problem is more difficult than the first one, you start taking note of this. You solve that one too.

You continue going in the same direction towards your goal, and if the third problem is more difficult than the second one, the system is telling you that this is not the direction to go.

But if the second problem is easier than the first one, and the third one is easier than the second one, then the system is telling you to go ahead, full speed ahead: you are on the right track.

Use your mind like this. You always must be aware of those conditions taking place while you are doing your thing, whatever that is.

Program for the Best Thing for Everyone Concerned

Always consider that the benefits are for more than just you. If it is only me, me, and you don't care about anybody else—big question mark.

And whenever you ask, remember: ask for no more than what you need, but do ask for no less than what you need. That's good enough.

What you need means, what plans do you have? Are they big plans? If so, you need something big. If they are little plans, you need something little.

Can You Program to Get a Rolls-Royce?

Sometimes a person will ask if you can program for a Rolls-Royce. This is in the possibility area.

But you see, we're not going to get help from the other side when we want something like this, only for me.

But if I say, "I want this vehicle, that we can use—*we*, not just me—because there is a need for something like this," and it's within the possibility area, and I don't have the means, I may then get the other side to help me.

The other side will only help me when I am asking for something that is needed to improve conditions on planet earth.

As we said, they are not going to help me if I want another million dollars when I already have a million dollars, when I want a Rolls-Royce when I have a Rolls-Royce already, when I want a girlfriend when I already have a wife. Some people ask for something like this.

Higher intelligence is not going to help you. You are on your own. If you make a mistake, you are going to suffer for it. You don't get help from the other side.

You only get help from the other side when your intentions are to help improve conditions on the planet for more than yourself, not just yourself.

If you only consider me, me, you have to do it on your own. If it is for us, if whatever you do is going to help more than just you, then you get help.

The more you are going to help, the more help you get for it.

So what your needs will be depends on how big your plans are. That's what your needs will be.

Use Your Successes to Bring about More Success

Go to alpha when you have succeeded. Go to alpha and strengthen the feeling of success, when you succeeded, the way you succeeded.

Go over whatever you did when you were successful, in order to reinforce it. That's a good foundation to keep on succeeding.

We used to say, "You reach success with a ladder of failures."

That's wrong.

We reach greater successes with a ladder of lesser successes. Always, your foundation should be success. Not failure.

So reinforce your successes to make them appear more frequently and stronger from here on. Reinforce at alpha your experiences of having succeeded.

Nobody will know the feeling of success until you succeed. There is no way to explain to anybody how it feels to succeed. It is a very unusual feeling, when you succeed.

Wisdom is the accumulation of feelings of success. That's wisdom: accumulation of feelings of success.

Part Two

Removing Impediments

5

Transforming Fear, Guilt, and Doubt

As long as you keep yourself centered, and are fulfilling the purpose you were sent here for, you will succeed and be prosperous in all areas of life.

—José Silva

Do you feel as if your subconscious has been kicking you around, impeding your opportunities to achieve the kind of success that you know, deep within yourself, that you are capable of and deserve?

Here is some good news:

By practicing the Silva Centering Exercise, you have now learned to use the so-called "subconscious" consciously.

But wait—that is a contradiction in terms, isn't it? If you can use those deep levels consciously, they are no longer "sub"—beneath—consciousness.

This is something new, that is not covered in conventional psychology, so José Silva coined a new term: instead of calling it the *subconscious*, he called it *the inner conscious level.*

You can enter the inner conscious level and rewrite your life history. You won't actually erase the old memories, but you can neutralize anything that is holding you back and impeding your progress.

Imagine how powerful a tool this is. Were you told—by people who had good intentions and were trying to motivate you—that in order to be successful in life, you had to make good grades?

If you are like most of us, then you probably made average grades, so if you learned to equate the amount of success you are allowed to have with the grades you made, no wonder you have had average success.

Did you ever make a mistake and hurt somebody without meaning to, and then feel guilty about it? That guilt can build and make us feel unworthy.

People who were sincerely trying to help us might have instilled irrational fears in our young, maturing brains, and those fears are now buried at deep levels that most people don't have access to.

Now you have access to those parts of the brain that were dominant when you were young: the alpha and theta levels, at lower brain frequencies.

You can access those levels any time you need them. Just close your eyes, take a deep breath, and while exhaling, dial 3–3–3, 2–2–2, 1–1–1, and you will be at your center, the alpha level, where you can start working to neutralize any limiting belief or old past programming that could be holding you back.

Now you can use your mind power to convert fear, guilt, and doubt into confidence, spontaneity, and hope, in order to dissolve problems by manifesting solutions. You can develop a charisma that radiates out and influences everyone and everything in your life.

Do you wish there had been more positive reinforcement in your life when you were young? Now you can go back and make it happen.

When you repeat beneficial statements like those in the Silva Centering Exercise while you are at deep levels of mind and low brain frequencies, it is like going back—from the point of view of the brain—to an earlier age and filling your life with those positive statements.

You can take positive action now to change your deep inner beliefs by using the Three-Scenes Technique that you learned in chapter 4.

You don't even need to know where the problem came from, how it developed, or why you have it. You don't need to know the exact nature of the problem.

All you need to know to get started is how the problem is affecting you today. When you visualize the problem you have now in the first scene, you are on your way to dealing with it at your inner conscious level.

Thanks to the new science of psychorientology—orienting the mind for greater success—that José Silva founded, we know that many of the things that most courses teach you about how to use your mind to solve problems are wrong and can actually make the problem worse.

As we mentioned in the previous chapter, the way to overcome a problem is to leapfrog over the problem, set your sights beyond it, and concentrate on solutions. We do identify and analyze the problem first so we understand it, but then we move forward and concentrate on the solution.

Everything begins with a thought. We move in the direction of our dominant thoughts. In other words: Mind guides brain, and brain guides body. Trying to untangle the problem and push your way through it just keeps your attention on the problem, and since we move in the direction of our dominant thoughts, we are stuck with the problem.

Beta Motivation Doesn't Work at the Alpha Level

To us, the law of attraction is BS, which means "beta stuff."

It may sound great to the left-brain hemisphere, at the outer—beta—brain-wave level, but it doesn't work. The slick talkers who can make anything sound exciting might convince people who are looking for a quick fix that your mind acts like a magnet and attracts things to you. There is no scientific evidence to support that, and it is the opposite of what we do.

The truth is that you can project your mind to find the solution to any problem, like a heat-seeking missile. Your mind acts like a guided missile, and once you give it a target, it will hone in and go after that target until it gets it, if it is within the possibility area.

That's why José Silva changed the meaning of ESP. *Extra-sensory perception* was too passive for him. We don't sit and wait for something to maybe come our way that might help us. We changed the meaning of ESP to *Effective Sensory Projection.*

You can project your mind effectively—and reliably—to find any answers you need, and to guide you to solutions to your problems.

It is all based on Mr. Silva's twenty-two years of scientific research, and we have dozens of scientific research studies to support us.

Mind guides brain and brain guides body.

We move in the direction of our dominant thoughts.

When the law of attraction people tell you to program that you are a confident person, that sounds good at the weak, outer, beta level, but at the strong, inner, alpha level—what some people call the subconscious—you know that you aren't a confident person, and you are just pretending you are. It reinforces the problem!

The solution is to concentrate on solving a problem. Use our techniques to increase your desire to solve that problem, and when your desire is strong enough, and your belief that this is the right thing to do for everybody concerned, and that you must somehow find a way to do it. Then confidence isn't even an issue; you just go at it and do it.

That is what really builds your confidence: success. The more successes you have, the more you believe in your own ability . . . and the more confident you are.

Let's take a look at how to overcome fear, guilt, and doubt, and convert them to courage, self-esteem, and self-confidence.

How to Overcome Irrational Fears

Let's look at fear first.

Fear is part of our survival mechanism. When a fear is rational, it can keep us from harm. For instance, if you are about to step off the sidewalk to cross the street and you hear a loud horn blow and jump back onto the sidewalk before a truck hits you, that's a good thing.

Irrational fear is *not* a good thing. Some people are afraid of confined places, and cannot ride on elevators. They might be so uncomfortable in small meeting rooms that it affects their jobs. Others have an irrational fear of being around a group of people. This fear prevents them from eating in restaurants, or from taking a self-improvement course like the Silva UltraMind ESP System.

You can have much more freedom in your life if you can eliminate—or at least control—irrational fears.

These fears are often rooted in our childhood. Many times they come from well-meaning adults who are trying to help us.

For instance, a grandmother sees her young granddaughter walking along a seawall as the surf crashes into it. She shouts at the toddler to get down immediately or she will be badly hurt. Grandmother is looking out for the child's safety, but to the child, this incident may very well create a fear of surf and water so that she will never feel safe around water.

A child being taken into a "haunted house" for the first time by his parents may become so frightened that from now on he is afraid of the dark.

Fears can grow on their own, and spread out. The youngster who is afraid of the dark might be afraid to get up during the night and answer the phone when it rings, and this can lead to an irrational fear of telephones.

The Guilt Complex

Guilt is another emotion that can lead to problems. We have all done things that we wish we hadn't done, and we feel bad about them. Up to a point, this can be a good thing, because it can make us more cautious in the future.

José Silva said that if something has survival value, then this is good. But if it doesn't have survival value, then you can enter your level and neutralize it.

Here are three questions you can ask yourself about guilt:

1. Did I learn a lesson from it? If not, then enter your level and learn what you did wrong, if anything. If you did nothing wrong, then there is no survival value in keeping the guilt.
2. Have you done what you can to make restitution? If not, can you do so now? If so, then do it. If there is no way to

make restitution, or if you have already done all that you can, then you can let it go; it has no more survival value.

3. Have you made a commitment that you will never do it again?

If you have taken care of these three issues, then there is no further reason to hold on to the guilt; it has no more survival value for you.

Correcting Problems

The way to deal with irrational fears, and also with guilt that no longer serves any useful purpose, is to enter your level and use the Three-Scenes Technique.

It has been said that we need to be able to love and respect ourselves before we can love and respect others. And that is the essence of all religions: Do unto others only what you want them to do to you. Love thy God with all thy heart and soul and mind, and love thy neighbor as thyself.

How can you love your God, whom you cannot see, if you cannot love and respect your neighbor—an example of the Creator's highest creation—whom you can see?

So program at your level to overcome fear, guilt, and doubt so that you can fulfill your mission in life.

Fear: In the first scene, visualize (recall) an irrational fear. In the second scene, imagine becoming more comfortable doing what you fear. In the third scene, imagine yourself facing that situation without fear.

Guilt: In the first scene, visualize (recall) the action that you feel guilty about. In the second scene, use your imagination to change it. In your imagination, in the third scene, do what you wish you had done, instead of what you did. Then take action in the physical world. Being active—serving a purpose that is bigger than yourself by helping others who need help without requiring or expecting anything in return—is very important. It is such a powerful healing strategy that it helps people who have experienced unimaginable traumas in their lives.

Wounded Warriors Heal by Helping Others

Combat veterans returning from war often experience posttraumatic stress disorder (PTSD). It can take years of conventional therapy to overcome it. But recently some organizations have found a nontraditional approach that produces startling results: instead of working on their own problems, individuals go out and help somebody else overcome their problem.

Sound familiar?

A report that aired in November 2016 on television station WRAL in North Carolina gave an example of one such operation. According to the report, former military members joined Team Rubicon, a volunteer organization mostly made up of military veterans, as well as first responders and some civilians, that was working to provide disaster relief in Goldsboro and other areas affected by Hurricane Matthew.

Organizers said the program helps veterans have a sense of purpose since entering the civilian workforce.

"It's amazing to see what we can do when we come together as a community," veteran volunteer Raswneet Bain said. "To know the skills we acquired while in the military, to know there's this opportunity to use those skills as a civilian to help out the community, what more could you want?"

Stephanie West, a veteran volunteer summed it up this way: "PTSD is something I deal with every day, doing projects like this with like-minded veterans, we heal each other and are always there for each other, it's great."

By the way, you don't have to be a combat veteran to realize the benefits of serving mankind.

José Silva said that we were sent here to improve conditions on planet earth. He told us that a human being is not one who *looks* like one, but one who *acts* like one. To qualify as humans, he said, you must take part in humanitarian activities.

It makes no sense for humans to believe that they should be destroying the creatures created by the Creator; the Creator is a creator, not a destroyer, he pointed out.

Instead of trying to fool yourself into believing that you are confident or worthy of praise, go out and *do something* that is worthy of praise.

If you don't love yourself, because of things in the past, because of fears, guilt, doubts, then take care of that. As someone once said, "If I am not for myself, how can anyone else be for me? And if I am only for myself, why should anyone else be for me?"

So get to work on it now. If not now, when? If not here, where?

José Silva's formula for correcting past mistakes and improving your confidence, self-image, and self-esteem is in the last paragraph given in the course, which you learned in chapter 2:

You will continue to strive to take part in constructive and creative activities to make this a better world to live in, so that when you move on, you shall have left behind a better world for those who follow.

Easy Does It

When programming to neutralize old fear and guilt, always start with the thing you are *least* afraid of, or the thing you feel the *least* guilty about.

As we mentioned earlier, our fears and our sources of guilt are usually linked to one another. When you start to neutralize them one at a time, this can affect them all.

If you neutralize a few of your fears, then you may find that the others fade away on their own.

The same with guilt. Rewrite the script for a very small thing you feel guilty about, then another, and another, and soon you will find that you do not have much to feel guilty about.

And as you neutralize your fears and your guilt, you will find your self-doubt going away too as you develop confidence and a whole new attitude about yourself.

Tips to Help You Succeed

Here are some more tips for using the Three-Scenes Technique to banish irrational fear, guilt, and doubt.

Fear: Take the thing you fear the least and program it. In the first scene, visualize yourself in the frightening situation. In the second scene, imagine yourself in that situation, not afraid but confident. Then in the third scene, picture yourself in the situation with total confidence. Remember, always program for perfection, and be grateful for any progress you make. After you have banished the least threatening fear, do the same with the next least threatening fear.

Guilt: If you have done something that you feel guilty about, make a good study of it in the first scene. Have you made restitution? Then picture yourself in the second scene doing so, and also do so objectively—that is, in the external, physical world—if you can. Have you learned your lesson from this mistake? If not, learn it. Have you made a commitment not to make that mistake again? Make that commitment. If you have done those things, there is no need to keep the guilt any longer, so in the second scene, change what happened; replay the event with a different outcome. You have learned your lesson, you now know a better way to handle the situation, so do so in the second scene. Neutralize the guilt.

Then in the third scene, picture yourself happy and content, knowing that you are a better person because of the way you have handled the situation and the lessons you have learned.

Doubt: When you deal with irrational fears and guilt in this manner, you will find that your doubts begin to fade away by themselves, even without programming them.

Here are some specific case studies of how Silva graduates overcame various impediments to their success.

Programming Overcomes Lifelong Fear of Flying

Have you ever seen someone with a fear of flying? It can paralyze them, make them physically ill.

Allen Rose, a columnist with a central Florida daily newspaper, had been plagued with fear of flying for more than thirty years. Then he learned the Silva System.

"I had tried everything," he recalled. "I had read every book on the subject I could find. Even called a guy halfway across the country who taught a course for white-knucklers. I knew all of the statistics about airplanes being the safest way to go. Nothing worked. I had to almost soak myself in alcohol to go near a plane."

Even though his logical beta mind knew that flying was safer than riding in a car, he was still plagued with that irrational fear at a deep inner level.

After Rose knew how to enter his inner conscious level and create new inner images of himself being confident in that situation, he eliminated that fear.

"Since the Silva course," he wrote in his newspaper column, "I have taken four flights. Couldn't wait to get aboard the last one. Now, I wouldn't hesitate to jump on a jet tomorrow for any place in the world. And that, friend, is a circumstance I had long ago considered impossible in this life."

A Simple Technique to Banish Fear

Allen Rose's Silva instructor, Betty Perry, explained that he used "a very simple technique to overcome his fear of flying.

"I suggested something I had read about in the *Silva Newsletter*," she said. "José Silva said if you have a fear, admit to the fear and it will never happen again."

"I've told many people to use this technique for fears, and they've been very successful," Perry said.

Do you ever get nervous when you are around other people, or have to talk with them?

Consider the story of a lady who had agoraphobia when she came to the Silva course.

"She would get anxiety attacks in public places," Perry said. "The first weekend of the class, she stayed in her room to eat. Then she used the technique to get over her fear.

"The second weekend, she ate in a restaurant for the first time in four years."

The story gets better. "When I called to see if she was going to repeat the next class," Perry said, "she said, 'I can't.' I asked what she meant. She told me she was taking a trip to Panama. When I asked who was going with her, she indignantly said, 'By myself!'"

Mental Rehearsal

Here's another self-programming technique that you can use to correct problems and achieve goals.

This technique—the Silva Mental Rehearsal Technique—is for practicing skills mentally, so that you can perform them better physically.

You can use this in addition to the Three-Scenes Technique, or instead of it. As always, let your results guide you.

When you use the Three-Scenes Technique, you step outside of the scene, so to speak, and observe the scene. By doing this, you can watch yourself in a detached manner. It is like watching a movie of yourself.

With the Mental Rehearsal Technique, you are totally involved. You are right there doing it—not observing yourself doing it, but *doing* it.

For instance, let's say that you want to program yourself to be more assertive. You can use either technique:

- You can use visualization and imagination with the Three-Scenes Technique. Create a picture of the problem in the first scene. It can be a moving picture. Then, after making a good study of the problem—by observing how you act and react—you move to the second and third scenes to correct the problem.

- With the Mental Rehearsal Technique, you can go back to the actual situation. You can relive it, go through the experience again. Then you can imagine acting differently—you can imagine being more assertive. This can be very beneficial, because you are doing it mentally, with your imagination, instead of physically, with another person involved.

The Three-Scenes Technique is like watching a movie of somebody else doing it. The Mental Rehearsal Technique is like doing it yourself. In one case, you are the audience; in the other, you are the participant.

With the Mental Rehearsal Technique, you may find it easier to get your feelings involved.

- Recall the feeling of being intimidated, for instance, if this happens to you.
- Then, as you rehearse mentally—or use the Three-Scenes Technique—imagine the feeling you get when you stand up for yourself.

Program Yourself to Perform Activities Better

We also teach this Mental Rehearsal Technique in the Silva Star Athlete program. It is a wonderful way to improve physical skills, such as athletic performance.

If you are going to use it to improve your athletic performance, then, before you even enter your level to program and to rehearse mentally, first make strong points of reference about every aspect of the task as you perform it physically. Get your coach to help you.

You can actually go to the place where you practice, and go through a practice session. Pay special attention to how you feel as you go through each moment. Make an impression of how it feels when you are one-fourth through the movement. Make an impression of how it feels when you are halfway through the movement or exercise. Then again three-quarters of the way through, and again at the completion of the movement.

If you want to improve your golf swing, first you will physically make an impression of exactly how it feels when you address the ball.

How does it feel when you start your backswing? Halfway through your backswing? At the top of your backswing?

Make these impressions throughout your swing, as you are actually swinging the club.

When you do this, have your coach there to make sure that you are doing it correctly.

Repeat this for every movement: your chip shots, putts, and so on.

Make impressions of where you are now, and where you want to go. Then at your level, you can imagine yourself correcting mistakes and improving your performance.

Keep making these impressions as you go, impressions at each step. Later, just recall the feeling, and you will be there, feeling as though you have practiced, as though you had actually done the movements, even though you only did them at your level.

Once you have made the impressions physically, then you can practice at any time you desire, even lying in bed. By doing this, you get the benefits of practice, but without fatiguing your body.

While at your level, bring back and visualize the feeling that you had when you performed the movements physically, and your body will respond the same way.

It is important to get your feelings involved. This is a very powerful way to program.

In order to make strong impressions of the special feeling of success, whenever you have a success, as soon as possible, enter your level, and while at your level, review your performance and recall how you felt when you were successful. This will help you to be even more successful in the future.

Use Any Technique That Solves the Problem

You can mix and match techniques, and find what works best for you. You can always start with the Three-Scenes Technique to program your desired end result, and then use Mental Rehearsal to help you achieve it.

For instance, if you are in sales, you can use the Three-Scenes Technique to imagine yourself being named Salesperson of the Year, and imagine your picture in the company newsletter, getting the award. Imagine watching a video of yourself getting this award.

Then you can use Mental Rehearsal to improve your selling skills. You can program yourself to help you stay calm, or be enthusiastic—whatever you need—and to project a confident image when you are working. Or to remind yourself that your main goal is to help your customer, and to be fairly compensated for doing so.

How Feedback Helps You

If you program for something and you encounter a problem, solve the problem and continue on.

When you encounter another problem, solve it and continue on.

But notice if it took *longer* to solve the second problem than the first. If it did, take note of that.

When you encounter a third problem, if it takes twice as long to solve it as it did to solve the second problem, and it took twice as long to solve the second one as the first, then higher intelligence might be telling you that you are going in the wrong direction.

On the other hand, if the second problem takes only half as long to solve as the first, and the third takes only half as long as the second, then continue on, full speed ahead. Higher intelligence is telling you that you are on the right track. Keep on going.

Self-Confidence, Self-Esteem

There are two very simple things you can do to increase self-confidence:

1. Make sure that all your inner images are positive. Cancel, erase, delete, or banish negative images and replace them with positive inner images.
2. Keep all statements and objective actions positive.

When you work from the inside out—maintaining positive inner images of what you desire—and from the outside in—"fake it till you make it"—then any doubt in the middle will be squeezed out.

All parts of the brain know what is going on.

The key to doing this on your own is as follows:

1. Practice the Silva Centering Exercise correctly to deepen your level. Go directly to the source by using this exercise,

and make changes on the inside. You may think that this is boring. Well, it is. It is designed to be boring, so that you can tune out exciting and interesting outside activities and go within and focus on the underlying characteristics that cause you to do the things you do.

2. Make changes from within simply by changing your inner images. Use the Three-Scenes Technique to change anything you want to change. Program yourself that any time you experience a negative thought or negative inner image, you erase it quickly and immediately recall and visualize the positive image framed in white.

This is why you see so many athletes talk about how great they are and what they are going to accomplish. Every good athlete concentrates mentally on correct performance. The inner images that these athletes have are images of performing correctly, the way they have been taught and coached to do. Their statements are consistent with this goal, even if they don't really believe them.

Athletes who try to avoid mistakes are focusing on the mistakes, both with their inner images and with their words. And their deeds are consistent with these: it is the mistakes that manifest.

We move in the direction of our dominant thoughts. We need to keep our thoughts (inner images) plus our words and our deeds (outer actions) consistent—and positive.

When you do something, do you do it hoping it will turn out right? Or do you have a "fake it till you make it" attitude and perform as if you are going to succeed?

Put on the "squeeze play." Let both the subconscious and the conscious mind know what you want to happen. They will come together and squeeze out any doubt, any tendency towards mistakes, self-sabotage, errors, and failure.

When you have an inner image of success and achievement, when you talk about achieving your goals, and when you act as if you are going to achieve success, the squeeze play goes into action and squashes doubts and insecurities and fears. Your brain has no choice but to send the correct signals to all parts of your body so that you achieve what you desire.

This is just as true in getting a date, talking to the most popular kid in school, impressing a potential employer, or remembering your studies and acing a test, as it is in athletic performance, learning to dance, performing in a music group, or any other physical activity.

One of our greatest fears—speaking in public—or sometimes just speaking to one special person—is overcome by exactly this approach. Create strong inner images of what you desire, then act as if you already have all the confidence in the world. Act, think, and feel the way you would act, think, and feel if you had done this thousands of times before . . . and you will do it.

Pretend you are an actor, playing the part of somebody who is recognized as the greatest in this field, and do what that person would do. If you do and say the things that the world's greatest would do and say, then you will appear to actually be the world's greatest. And when people respond as though you really are great, this will reinforce your feelings of success and achievement.

Correcting the Cause of the Problem

You might be wondering how you can correct a problem when we keep emphasizing that we don't work on problems, we concentrate on solutions instead.

If we are not dealing with the problem directly, won't it continue to cause us problems on our future projects?

With almost any other system, that would be true. A hypnotist can program you while you are hypnotized and get rid of your problem, but this will not correct the cause of the problem. As a result, you will continue to experience problems.

However, when you enter your level yourself, on your own, and you apply the formula and do the work yourself, then what you are doing is telling your mind to correct the cause of the problem.

Then your mind will do whatever is necessary to correct the cause of the problem. You may not ever be aware of what was done to correct the cause of the problem, but your mind knows.

This is what makes José Silva's System different from any other program in history: It gives you a means of taking care of your own problems at the source. It puts you in charge of your own life.

Nobody else can do it for you as well as you can do it for yourself—provided that you apply the techniques at the alpha level.

A former Silva instructor named Tag Powell loved to sum this up with ten little two-letter words:

If it is to be, it is up to me.

Begin Today

You now have in your hands the power to change your life.

You now have the tools that you need to choose success.

Review this book from time to time. Review all of the techniques, and use them at every opportunity.

And most importantly: practice, practice, practice.

Remember what your purpose is: to help correct problems on the planet. Including your own problems, of course, so that you will be a better problem solver. You must prepare the vehicle. You are a vehicle, and in order to be the best problem-solving agent that you can be, you need to have your own life under control.

But that is only a step along the way, a means to an end.

Always keep in mind one of José Silva's most important guiding principles: that we were sent here to correct problems and to improve living conditions on planet earth. Program to correct a problem that affects both you and someone else. Program for both of you. For all of you.

Enter your level every day: once, twice, three times a day. Also get out into the world and apply yourself. You must have feedback to know that your programming is working.

If you program to be more confident, then go out and be more confident.

Let your results guide you. Program in a manner such that you would expect to see some kind of progress, some result, within two or three days.

If things get better, then you know that you are on the right track. That's the way that our helpers on the other side let us know that we are going in the correct direction.

6

Eliminating Blocks to Your Success

Being a collector of insights is not sufficient; utilizing insights for the betterment of self and humanity are more worthwhile projects.

—JOSÉ SILVA

Everything you have ever experienced, from the womb until now, has been impressed on your brain neurons and therefore has altered your brain. This includes everything you have seen and heard and felt as well as every thought you have had.

Scientists who study the brain have confirmed that all of these things actually alter the brain physically. They create new synaptic connections that can last a lifetime.

We continue to learn new things throughout our lives, of course. People have learned to paint and sing and play musical instruments late in life, after they retired, even though they had never been exposed to these activities previously.

The brain is like a computer that is constantly and automatically updating its software.

Healing the Wounded Child Within

Many books have been written and seminars presented during the last few decades about "healing the wounded child within." The books and seminars and support groups have helped a lot of people, but not everybody finds the solutions they are seeking. Many are still seeking.

The problem is that children don't have the capacity to analyze information the way grown-ups do, so they simply accept the things they are told and the experiences they have as truth.

There is a big difference between discipline and punishment. Discipline is sometimes appropriate in order to help the child learn. Punishment is almost always harmful.

If the child was told, "You are bad!" rather than being told, "What you did was bad," that was what was impressed on that part of the brain. If that message is reinforced too many times, then the brain—the "inner child"—accept it as reality. As a result, the child might be afraid to take action for fear of hurting someone because they "know" that "I am a bad person."

This can affect your decisions and actions today. Those inner feelings could stop you from acting at all, or could cause you to act in a fearful, tentative way, because deep within, you still have that fear that you are a bad person who does things that hurt people, and are then punished for it.

People will sense that in you, and will be reluctant to interact with you. It will be difficult for you to develop leadership characteristics. Why would anybody want to follow the lead of a person like that?

You are a good person. You have accumulated information and experiences that make it obvious that you are a good person who helps people, but that information and those experiences are impressed on the "adult" part of your brain.

Here is the question that has baffled so many people:

If you know that the old information was faulty and that you are, in fact, a good person, then why does the old experience still cause you problems today?

This was not a subject that José Silva dealt with specifically. He was more interested in doing constructive and creative things rather than dwelling on the past. But the way he lived his life gave us an excellent example of what you can do today to overcome impediments to your success.

How Humans Develop

The understanding you have now, as an adult, is impressed on a different part of your brain.

José Silva used his own ten children as research subjects, and learned a lot about how humans develop. He explained:

We grow in life cycles of seven years per life cycle. The first seven life cycles are called *anabolic* cycles, because we grow, we gain. Every time we gain in a cycle, it is called *anabolic*; every time we lose in the cycle is called *catabolic*. So we grow through so many anabolic cycles in human development of the brain.

During the first seven-year life cycle, the mind functions only inductively, meaning the child has no ability to analyze. The child knows things happen, but doesn't know why. The child has no means to try to figure out why things happen or the reason for it. So the analytical processes, the critical consciousness, is not there yet.

Of course, the brain functions in the complete spectrum, but the child is spending more time at lower brain frequencies.

Now the overall average of the brain frequency of a child is always lower than the overall average brain frequency of a mature adult.

In the second seven-year anabolic cycle in life, between the ages of seven and fourteen, we develop the analytical mind, critical consciousness. The analytical processes come on the scene, meaning the deductive faculty of mind comes on the scene.

This is the human intelligence region; the alpha brain frequency region is the highest human intelligence level, where we start to analyze problems.

Different Modes of Learning

Once you understand how humans develop, it is easy to see what the problem is:

At the time the child received the faulty information, the child could only function inductively, meaning the child had no ability to analyze the information. The child knew that things were happening, but didn't know why. The child had no means to try to figure out why things happened, because the analytical process, the critical consciousness, was not there yet.

The understanding you have now, as an adult, is impressed on a different part of your brain.

That leaves you, as an adult, trying to reason logically with an inner child who doesn't yet have the ability to reason logically.

You need to demonstrate it in a way that the child can believe. Remember, the information is stored in a part of the brain that doesn't have "critical consciousness." That's why explanations don't work, no matter how logical they are.

It was action that created the old negative belief, and it will take action to alter it, or neutralize it.

The adult cannot reason with the inner child. The adult must take action to show the child that the child is not bad, but is OK.

You can approach this both mentally and physically, and your mind will figure out how to resolve it.

Creating a Different Reality for a Six-Year-Old Child

José Silva dealt with early traumatic experiences instinctively, with great results. His father was killed in a terrorist act when José was just four years old. When he went to visit his father in the hospital, he saw him lose consciousness. He died soon after.

Two years later José's mother remarried and moved away, leaving six-year-old José as the eldest male in the family.

Most children who lose parents at an early age feel a great sense of abandonment and shame. They wonder if it was their fault that their parents went somewhere else rather than staying with the child. This was a question that haunted José for years after he saw his father faint: "What happened to him, where did he go, and what did he do, when he fainted?"

He refused to accept his bleak circumstances, and took action to create another reality than the one he found himself in. His uncle made him a shoeshine box, and he went to work shining shoes and doing whatever else he could do that would have value to people.

In this way, at six years old, he demonstrated to himself that his life had value. Many people were willing to pay him for his services. This attitude eventually led to a surprising benefit.

When Mr. Silva was in his thirties, he got the answer to the six-year-old child's question when himself fainted one day. When his family heard him fall, they came rushing to see what had happened and saw a strange sight:

"They saw me sitting on the floor, smiling," he said. "My wife was crying, and demanded: 'Why do you smile?' I answered, 'Now I know how fainting feels: you feel nothing!'" His inner child now knew that his father hadn't abandoned him for something better.

He said that he became more serious about life and accomplishing things after that experience. "It is like I was a different person," he said.

This combination of physical action to demonstrate what it is you desire to be, along with rewriting your life history at deep levels of mind, seems to be the key to overcoming whatever faulty programming and traumatic events you may have encountered when you were young.

Three Steps toward Changing Old Inner Images

The way to convince the inner child that the old experiences were wrong is to *show* the child. Words and logical arguments are for grown-ups, for the adult part of the brain. We need to use mental pictures and emotions for the inner child.

Let's begin by making sure that the logical adult understands and accepts that the old lessons and experiences were faulty. To do this, enter your level, do some deepening exercises, and then analyze what happened to the child.

Sometimes this is all that it takes. Understanding the root of the problem might provide insights that solve the problem.

That happened to Ed Bernd Jr., who recalls:

Back when I was training to become a Silva instructor, I was sometimes asked to get up in front of a class and explain a technique. I was always very nervous when I was speaking to a group of people. I persisted despite my nervousness and fear because I wanted people to have the benefits of the Silva techniques.

Then one day, while at my level, I asked myself why I was so nervous. The answer that came to me was that I didn't want to be ridiculed. So I asked why I was so afraid of being ridiculed.

An answer came: Because when I was just barely six years old and had just started first grade, I had to wear high-topped corrective shoes because of the polio I'd had, and the other children teased and ridiculed me because of the shoes, and because I couldn't run as fast as they could.

I thought to myself: "That's a six-year-old's reaction; why am I still reacting that way now that I am thirty-six years old?" That was the end of the problem. I have not had any stage fright since. The bigger the audience is, the happier I am. I feel like I am at a party.

I was also taking action in the physical world and programming mentally, as I described in detail in chapter 5, and those actions paved the way and created the environment that allowed the insight to come to me.

Something else happened later that I found very interesting: Someone I was talking with mentioned how he had been teased when he was six years old, and I realized that *every* kid gets teased and ridiculed. There wasn't anything special about me. But that didn't matter, because it had solved my problem.

Once the adult is convinced that the old information was faulty, it will be easy to take the second step:

Take action to demonstrate to the inner child that the adult the child has grown into is a good person who deserves to be loved and respected.

To do this, just take part in constructive and creative activities that will help to solve problems and improve living conditions in order to make the world a better place to live.

Use your level to analyze problems that you become aware of and think of things you can do to help solve them, and program to correct them. Then get your body into motion and go out and do something to solve the problem.

Erase "Failures" and Dwell on Your Successes

The third thing you can do is to create a receptive environment that will enable the inner child to accept the new information.

One way to do this is to enter your level after you have succeeded at solving a problem and review your success. There are many benefits to doing this.

Entering your level and reviewing your success makes it easier for you to have future successes. For one thing, your belief in your ability to succeed will be strengthened. This will make it easier for you to have another success, which in turn will make it easier for you to believe you can succeed—it is like an endless self-reinforcing loop.

When you review your successes at your level, the inner child becomes aware of what a good person you are, a person who deserves love and respect.

If you came up short of the success you desired, then use the Three-Scenes Technique to change the "failure" into a success. Visualize (recall) the "failure" in the first scene, then erase it and move on to the second scenes, towards your left, and use your imagination to succeed. Then in the third scene, still further to your left, recall the special feeling of success.

Remember to make mental pictures of your successes. Make mental movies. Also recall the special feeling that comes with success. Children learn through observation, and emotion. So make mental movies, and recall the wonderful feelings of success and satisfaction.

Rewrite Your Personal History

You can also go back on the scale of brain evolution to a time—brainwise—when you were young, and rewrite any part of your personal history that you feel is holding you back. The Three-Scenes Technique is excellent for this.

You can create mental movies with alternative experiences. This won't erase the old impressions that were made on your brain neurons many years ago, but it will help to neutralize them and counterbalance them.

Remember that you also need to take action. Taking these steps—adult analysis and programming, coupled with action, along with creating mental movies of good things at deep levels of mind—will help you become more confident, better able to influence people, and happier. You will be a better friend, someone people want to be with,

Will it eliminate the old wounds and frustrations completely? Perhaps not. José Silva still had such strong emotions eighty years after his father was killed that he specified in his will that in lieu of flowers, donations be made to the local orphanage.

While those old feelings might have still been with him eight decades later, there were also many positive emotions and experiences that made his life a life well-lived.

Healing Unseen Wounds of Loss and War

Prof. Clancy D. McKenzie, MD, was one of the first to investigate José Silva's work to see if it would help his psychiatric patients. It did. He treated many military veterans who had fought in the Vietnam War and were suffering from PTSD. Many of them were able to gain insights at the alpha level that brought them immediate benefits that could have taken months or years with conventional therapy, Dr. McKenzie said.

One of the most valuable techniques was a variation of José Silva's Dream Control technique. Dr. McKenzie expanded on José Silva's "programmed dreams" formula, based on his experiences with his patients, in order to insure that you receive specific guidance on how to solve your problem. Here is how he explains it:

Utilizing the techniques, you will be able to spend one minute prior to going to bed to formulate a question, and one minute when you awaken to retrieve the answer.

There are two techniques I use. The first technique is to decide to have a dream about a specific problem, and that the *interpretation* of the dream will tell me exactly what to do. Add: "I will awaken at the very end of the dream, remember it, and write it down."

The second technique is to decide the mind will work on a particular problem throughout sleep, and that when you awaken, your first thought will be the answer.

Be sure to have pencil and paper nearby, and when you wake up start writing about your dream even before you open your eyes.

This technique is so powerful that it can sometimes solve the problem without conscious involvement.

"One combat veteran, for example, was having terrifying nightmares nearly every night," Dr. McKenzie recalled. "I prescribed a programmed dream to get rid of the nightmares. When he returned the next month his wife came with him. He complained that he didn't even have a dream, his wife quickly interjected: 'Yeah, but you haven't had any of those nightmares since!' So quickly it was resolved!"

Gaining Insights from Your Dreams

Dreams are like postcards from your subconscious. They can give you a lot of information about yourself, about how you think, about the things you like and dislike.

"I found that the same dream programming that helped the combat veterans deal with their PTSD also worked for everything else just as well," Dr. McKenzie said. "You can use programmed dreams to find solutions to problems with children, employment, income, where to live, and more." Here are some examples from Dr. McKenzie:

One of my patients wanted to be manager of a very large coat factory. He had applied almost two years earlier but had no response. I had him program a dream about getting the job, and within one week he was called and told he could have it.

At one time, I was thinking about purchasing a piece of land in Maryland near where they were building the new Bay Bridge. The sales pitch was, "When the Bay Bridge opens, the price is going to double, so buy two pieces of property and sell the second to pay for the first." I programmed a dream and the dream told me: "'When the Bay Bridge opens, everyone is going to want to sell their second piece of property to pay for the first, and the price will plummet!' That is exactly what happened. Other buyers lost money, but not me."

I am excited by a new realization as to why there are so many "coincidences" that follow the programmed dreams. For example, one patient wanted to teach school but did not have sufficient courses to get the teacher's certificate. I told her, "No problem; I'll write the dream programming." I wrote: "I will have a dream about teaching school, and the interpretation of the dream will tell me exactly what to do."

She didn't remember the dream, but the next morning she decided to go for a walk, and she walked in a neighborhood where she never had been. Then she saw a lady scrubbing windows outside a house and recognized her as an old friend of her mother. She invited her in, and while they were sipping coffee, the friend said to her: "You'll never guess what I do. I'm teaching school. I didn't have enough college credits to get the teaching certificate, so I am teaching in the Catholic schools, where it is not necessary!"

Another lady wanted to get a job in the housekeeping department of the Marriott Hotel, so I had her program a dream. She didn't remember the dream, but she decided to take a bus into town. Philadelphia is a big city, millions of people. By "coincidence" an old friend boarded the bus and said, "Hi, girlfriend. What are you doing these days?" The patient replied, "I'm looking for a job in the housekeeping department of the Marriott Hotel." Her friend replied, "Girl, this is your lucky day. I'm the supervisor of the housekeeping department at the Marriott Hotel, and I am looking to fill three positions."

I believe what this confirms for us is that this is a direct communication from the Father. He not only gives us the answers in the dreams, but when he sees a quicker way to implement the solution, He does it. As José Silva used to say, "Coincidences are God's way of showing His hand."

When you program long enough for dreams, the mind becomes aware that you want to gather information during sleep, and it automatically does this for you. And the information reaches beyond the dreamer, and beyond information that you would presume is contained in the mind.

Dr. McKenzie said that some of the combat veterans he was working with didn't remember any dreams even after programming to do so. He told them that when they woke up in the morning, they were to sit up in bed (so they wouldn't fall back to sleep) and imagine what kind of dream they *would have* had, what kind of information they *would have* gotten.

When somebody said he couldn't imagine anything, Dr. McKenzie would tell him to just make something up. It worked: whatever they made up usually gave them an insight that helped them.

Dr. McKenzie said that when they did the work themselves and obtained their own insights, the insights they got were often enough to bring about great improvement in their condition and their lives. They often got results in a matter of days that could have taken many months or even years with conventional therapy.

How to Interpret Your Dreams

Many times dreams are more symbolic than literal, so how do we go about interpreting the dreams and understand the symbolism?

We don't do it by picking up a cheap book in the grocery-store checkout lane. Dreams tend to be very personalized, and the same symbols and actions can mean very different things to different people.

What you need to do is to write down the dream—make some notes about it *as soon as you have it*. That is very important. The dream may be so vivid that you are sure you will never forget it. That is an illusion. Until you put the dream into some physical form—writing it down, or speaking into a voice recorder—it can vanish in a second.

Dreams occur at high alpha, around 14 cycles per second, so the best place to recall your dream and to analyze it is the same place where you had it: alpha.

Think about things that happened the previous day, and see if anything in the dreams seems to relate to any of those things. You will begin to see patterns, and this will help you to understand and interpret your dreams. It is all very personal to you.

There are many good books about dreams where you can learn more. They can give you general guidelines on the meaning of certain themes, but not on specific symbols. If the author tries to tell you what specific things symbolize, look for another book.

Everybody Can Benefit from These Techniques

If the Silva System is powerful enough to empower severely disturbed patients to help themselves deal with their problems successfully, can you imagine how it can help people who are starting from a much stronger place? Even high achievers like Dr. McKenzie can benefit from it.

Dr. McKenzie told us that the creative insights he gained at the alpha level helped him to understand that experiences his patients had in childhood contributed to their depression, psychosis, and schizophrenia.

"Psychosis can be likened to most natural processes that have an origin, a triggering mechanism, and facilitating mechanisms," Dr. McKenzie explained. "All psychotics we have treated became ill as a result of a real or imagined rejection, separation, threatened loss, diminished attention, etc., triggering an unconscious fear of abandonment that related to back to an early childhood experience.

"The treatment methods based on that insight are so effective that many patients no longer need medication after the first few months."

In chapter 13 we will explore that in more depth, including advice and guidance on how to ensure that you raise healthy children.

Beneficial Statements to Help You Neutralize Impediments

When you enter deep levels of mind, you begin to ventilate the impediments that are stored there. Even if you don't do anything but enter your level for fifteen minutes, you begin to neutralize them.

When you saturate all levels with the beneficial statements that we use in the conditioning cycles, then you begin to neutralize the negative information stored at those deep levels.

Imagine the benefits when you go to very deep levels and mentally repeat statements like:

- Every day in every way I'm getting better, better and better.
- My increasing mental faculties are for serving humanity better.
- Positive thoughts brings me benefits and advantages I desire.
- And then there is the final statement in the course: *You will continue to strive to take part in constructive and creative activities . . .* and you have *greater understanding, compassion, and patience with others.*

Imagine how people will respond to you when you have saturated yourself at all levels with thoughts like those.

Those are not like the beta "affirmations" that some people try to sell us. Our Beneficial Statements do not concentrate on the problem, and they do not ask us to say anything about ourselves that we don't believe.

You can also take an active role in changing the stored information. You can install new information, new programs that will direct you towards success in your life.

You can use the Three-Scenes Technique that you learned in chapter 4 to correct problems from the past, to get rid of irrational fears, of old guilt, of doubt, and program yourself for greater success in your life today and in the future.

It all begins by preparing a proper foundation: establishing a deep, healthy level of mind, where you can function with conscious awareness.

How to Create a Burning Desire at Deep Inner Levels of Mind

Whenever you practice entering your level, it is important to have a reason for doing this. You must establish your purpose. Think about the benefits you will receive. Think about how you will be fulfilling your purpose, your mission here on earth. Think about all of the people who will benefit when you become a better problem solver, when you are helping to correct problems and make the world a better place to live.

You have already indicated that you have a great desire to help by committing the time to read this book and learn this System. That is a good indication of your desire. Now it is time to build on that desire, to increase it, and to transfer it gradually to lower brain frequencies, with conscious awareness.

The lower you take that desire, without altering it, the stronger it gets. Then you can use all of the energy of that desire in your programming.

The desire that you build up when you think of all of the reasons that you have for practicing will give you an extra boost, so that you will do whatever is necessary to succeed.

In addition, when you carry that sense of purpose to level with you, then you are taking your desires and your hopes and dreams to those deep levels with you, and that is very powerful. It is good to have hopes and dreams at the outer level; it is even better to take them to the powerful inner levels.

And when you have all of that desire, deep within, to correct problems, to help make the world a better place to live, then just imagine how people will respond to you as you express all of that desire from deep within yourself.

- People will want to be around you.
- They will want to be your friend.
- They will want to do business with you.

So work on your desire; review your reasons for wanting to banish impediments to your success. Make sure you have your priorities and your sense of values right.

Nobody Can Help You More than You Can Help Yourself

There is a special way to practice the Silva Centering Exercise to get maximum results.

Here's how *not* to do it: Do not just lie back and listen to somebody read the Silva Centering Exercise to you. Don't ask somebody else do all the work. That won't do you a whole lot of good.

You need to do it yourself.

Nobody else can do it for you, because:

- Nobody else knows how long it takes you to relax.
- Nobody else knows how tense you are.
- Nobody else knows what parts of your body you need to relax.
- Nobody else knows what you need, as well as you know.
- Nobody else knows where you hurt.
- Nobody else knows how much you hurt.

When you memorize the steps in the Silva Centering Exercise and practice on your own, do it for yourself, through your own efforts, then you'll be transferring that desire to those deep levels, and your desire at those deep levels will produce fabulous results.

It is very important that you get involved in the process.

It is important that you concentrate your sense of awareness on your scalp, the skin that covers your head.

It is important for you to mentally detect a fine vibration, a tingling sensation, a feeling of warmth caused by circulation. Use your imagination to help you do that. What would it feel like? Remember that you "detect" with your mind, and that you might not experience the fine vibration or tingling sensation or feeling or warmth when you are first learning, but you *will* begin to experience them if you continue to practice.

It is important that you then release and completely relax all tension and ligament pressures from this part of your head, and place it in a deep state of relaxation, that will grow deeper as you continue. Don't hold anything back, just let go and relax.

You then continue and do the same all the way down your body: your forehead, your eyes and the tissue surrounding your eyes, your face . . . the skin covering your cheeks, your throat and within the throat area, your shoulders, your chest, within the chest area, your abdomen, within the abdominal area, your thighs, the bones within the thighs, your knees, your calves, your feet.

Then come back up the body, and become so relaxed that you lose all sensation. Cause your feet to feel as though they do not belong to your body. Cause your feet, ankles, calves, knees, thighs, waist, shoulders, arms, and hands to feel as though they do not belong to your body.

Get involved, and cause it to happen.

Then relax mentally also by visualizing and recalling tranquil and passive scenes.

The more you practice, the easier it will be to do it.

At these deep levels we go back to our natural functions. Your body begins to normalize and function in a natural, healthy manner. We awaken intuition at these levels, and creativity.

Go at your own pace. Nobody knows better than you the best way for you to proceed. Make sure that you are comfortable with the experience. Continue practicing until you learn how to enter deep, healthy levels of mind, quickly and easily.

It is important that you continue to practice the Silva Centering Exercise regularly. We encourage Silva UltraMind System graduates to practice it once a week for three months after they graduate. Many of us continue to practice it at least once a week even after that.

If you do not continue to practice, then your level starts surfacing.

Practice helps ensure that when you go to level, you will stay there.

Do you know when the most important time to practice is? The most important time to practice is when you *don't* need to, when you are *not* under stress and will find it easy to relax. Then later, when you need to solve a difficult problem, going to your level will be automatic.

How Habits Can Improve Your Life

There is no such thing as a problem without a solution, only problems for which we do not yet have enough information to know what the solution is. When you have enough information, it is easy to solve a problem.

—JOSÉ SILVA

Habits can be your best friend—or your worst enemy.

There are bad habits, of course: eating or drinking too much, using drugs, and smoking in response to stress, for instance.

There are good habits also: brushing your teeth every night, and washing your hands before you eat.

We tend to do all of these things without thinking about them.

Let's talk first about what habits are, how to get rid of bad habits, and then how to create good new habits with actions and attitudes that will make you a more successful person.

Habits are patterns of behavior that are repeated over and over again until they become automatic. It is easier to do them than not to do them.

In other words, once you get used to doing something, any effort to change and do something else is very threatening. If you are accustomed to failing, the prospect of succeeding can be very threatening, so threatening that you find a way to fail.

The good news is that once you understand this, you can use the extra energy that's generated to your advantage, and turn fear into victory. Let's see how this works.

Habits are powerful because they build on a natural human trait: the apprehension that is triggered anytime we encounter something new or do something different. Or to say it more simply, fear of the unknown.

This apprehension creates energy that you can use to help you achieve your goals. Or it can create fear that can cause you to crawl in a hole and hide. The choice is yours. You can use this energy any way you desire.

Back before recorded history, in a time when our ancestors had to survive in the jungle, without tools or weapons, living by their wits, they developed very strong survival mechanisms.

Imagine them walking through the jungle and hearing a rustling in the bushes nearby. That noise could mean one of two things:

Perhaps it is a small animal, like a rabbit, that they can catch and eat.

Maybe it is a large animal, like a tiger, that wants to catch and eat them.

It is all a matter of survival. Catch the rabbit and eat it, and you will survive longer. Outrun the tiger, and you will survive.

Either way, our ancestors needed a big burst of energy. The people whose bodies could generate the most energy quickly in an emergency were the people who survived.

Their descendants—including you and me—inherited the characteristics of their ancestors, including the ability to create a lot of energy when something happens that they are not expecting, something new.

That's one reason that habits are so powerful: they are so familiar.

There are many habits that are very helpful to us. You probably don't even notice which leg you put into your pants first, or how you tie your shoelaces. These are things we do automatically, by habit. It makes life easier for us.

But some other habits are not so good for us.

All too often, people embrace habits that relate in some way to the survival mechanism, and use these habits to ease and reduce feelings of apprehension.

What are the greatest needs that we have in order to survive?

- We need food every few weeks.
- We need water every few days.
- We need air every few minutes.

When we feel threatened, we have a natural tendency to seek something to reassure us that we can continue to survive: so we ingest into our bodies food, liquids, air:

- Some people eat when they are under stress. High-calorie foods seem to work best—the ones high in sugars and fats— the ones that add the most weight—the ones that have little nutritional value.
- Some people drink when they are under stress. When they drink intoxicating liquids, then get the added benefit of a chemically induced feeling of euphoria. Sometimes they even drink themselves into a stupor, where they have no recollection of whatever is causing them stress.

- Some people seem to have such a great need for reassurance that they ingest smoke into their lungs, and when they breathe out, they can actually see their breath. No wonder smokers get so upset when you suggest that they stop smoking. Not only are they addicted to the nicotine, and to the physical movements involved—handling the cigarettes and so on—they also feel that we are attacking their breath, their very right to breathe! Well, we're not, of course.

Get Rid of Bad Habits

Now let's see what you can you get rid of bad habits and create helpful new habits.

José Silva has developed strategies to help you make the changes a little at a time. Small changes are usually easier to make than big ones. Instead of trying to deal with a big problem at all once, start by altering it. Keep making the problem smaller and smaller, and then it will be easier to eliminate it altogether.

Another strategy is to make the change mentally first, and then the physical change will be automatic.

Let's look at some specific examples, and then we will go to José Silva for the specific formula-type techniques that he developed. We will use the habits that José Silva identified and talked about, but this advice can be applied to all kinds of other habits.

The first step is always to enter your level, and at your level analyze the problem.

If the problem is cigarette smoking, for instance, then analyze and determine when you smoke the first cigarette of the day. Is it when you first wake up? With your cup of coffee? While you are on your way to work? Program yourself, at your level, to smoke the first cigarette one hour later.

You are not depriving yourself of the cigarette; you are just changing the habit. In effect, you are developing a new habit by smoking the first cigarette one hour later. And it is easier to break a new habit than an old one. An old habit is so familiar that it can be very difficult to part with. It is like a long-time love affair, and breaking up can be difficult. So do it little by little.

You can change habits in other ways too. For instance, smoke a different brand of cigarette. This makes it a new habit, which will be easier to break.

Here is a strategy that works for the most severe habits. We know people personally who had been addicted to heroin for several years and were able to stop using it in thirty days with this strategy:

First, mark a date on a calendar, thirty days from the present. Then enter your level and tell yourself mentally that on that date, you will stop smoking (or using drugs, or whatever habit you need to end), and will never smoke again in your life. Enter your level every day and reinforce this programming. When the thirty days are up, you will not want to smoke anymore.

You can apply this technique to any kind of habit.

Create Beneficial New Habits

You can create new habits in the same manner. Do them gradually.

If you want to get into the habit of going to level every morning when you first wake up, then in the beginning you might have to remind yourself to do it. You might have to rearrange your schedule a bit in order to do it. Make it easy on yourself by going to level for just five minutes.

When this becomes effective, then begin staying at level for ten minutes. When this is easy and natural, increase it to the recommended fifteen minutes.

Whenever you do something every day, you condition yourself to do it every day. You make it a habit. So pay attention to the habits you create, and make sure that all of your new habits are good habits.

What are the habits that successful people have?

Start studying successful people, the kind of people that you admire and would like to be like. What do they do? What are their regular habits?

Perhaps they get up earlier in the morning so that they can get some work done before other people start calling on them and interrupting them.

Maybe they have the habit of calling business associates or clients on a regular basis. Maybe they set aside fifteen minutes every day for such "service calls."

Maybe they exercise on a regular basis, because they know that in order to do the amount of work that they must do to achieve the level of success that they desire, they need a strong, healthy, and fit body.

Whatever habits they have, you can develop too.

Make the changes and start these news habits on the inside first by programming them at your level. Do them at level every day. This is easy; there is no stress involved. There is no stress when you imagine calling people on the phone. And after you get used to doing it at your level, you will find that it will be easy to do it objectively—physically—as well.

Program yourself at your level for thirty days to practice a regular exercise program. By that time, you will find that you are just as comfortable with the new habit that you have done at your level, as you are with the old habit, the physical habit. So it will be a simple choice. You can choose the habit that you want.

Imagination Always Beats Willpower

One word of caution: you cannot change habits with willpower.

Whenever willpower and imagination are in conflict, imagination always wins out.

Let's take a simple example: Suppose you are determined to eat better, to eat more nutritious food, so that you will remain healthy and will have the energy that you need to do the work that is required to be as successful as you desire. As always, it is your choice.

So you go into a diner with a group of friends. They all order big meals, but you only order the chef's salad, with the dressing on the side so that you won't consume too much high-calorie oil.

All goes well until time for dessert, when all of your friends order the big chocolate high-calorie goodie that looks so tempting . . . with the whipped cream . . . and the cherry on top . . . but you have willpower, so you are not going to order it . . . you are not going to . . . "Excuse me, waiter, would you bring me the same thing they are having?"

Your imagination got the best of you.

Use Your Imagination to Increase Your Willpower

The good news is that you can use your imagination to increase your willpower. At your level, program for what you desire. Get your imagination and your willpower working together.

You know how to master your imagination:

Dwell on what you desire: the good health, the feeling of energy.

Remember that we talked earlier about how important it is that you have a purpose, that you have reasons for doing what you are doing?

At your level, review the reasons that you have for wanting to change your eating habits, or to exercise more regularly, or to stop smoking or drinking or whatever it is you want to change. Then come up with more reasons.

Do it for your family's sake if you have no other reason. Do you want your children to imitate you and smoke, or drink, or lose their temper and get into trouble? Do you want to take the chance of having a heart attack, and having your family have to go on without you? This might be enough motivation for you to take whatever steps are necessary to change your habits.

Small Steps Lead to Big Successes

Remember what we mentioned about changing habits little by little.

Sometimes you might find it better to change only the part of the habit that causes the actual harm. That may be as far as you can go at that time.

José Silva suggests that if you are so accustomed to handling cigarettes with your hands, holding the cigarettes between your lips, and all of the little activities that are associated with cigarette smoking, then go ahead and do those things, but just don't inhale the cigarette smoke.

Drinkers can do the same thing by drinking nonalcoholic beer or wine. At first it may taste a little different, but before long you will grow accustomed to it.

José Silva suggests using a glass of tomato juice spiked with a liberal amount of hot pepper sauce whenever you have the urge to drink. Just be sure to consult with your doctor and make sure it is safe for you to use the hot sauce. Mr. Silva says that this is a good way to work on drinking and drug habits.

Have an "Instead-of" to Help You Change

Remember that when you want to end a habit, you are creating a vacuum in your life. Nature abhors a vacuum, so think of something you can use to replace the habit.

Replace the alcohol you have been drinking with a nonalcoholic beverage. Replace the cigarettes with three deep breaths. Inhale very deeply, so that you feel it in your lungs. This is a very effective "instead-of." Whenever you want to end a habit, review all of the suggestions in this chapter. Use any of them that seem reasonable to you. Analyze everything at your level, and get started.

There are many techniques and suggestions here, because each person is different and responds in a different way. Find something that works for you, and stick with it.

If one technique doesn't give you the results you want, try another one.

The choice is yours. If you really want to have more success in your life, then you will use the tools that we are providing in this book.

They work. If these techniques work for heroin addicts, for smokers, for alcoholics, then you can be confident that they will work for you too.

Effectiveness with Alcoholics

Research was conducted on the effectiveness of these techniques, applied at the alpha level, with recovering alcoholics living in a treatment facility.

In one research project, fifteen recovering alcoholics in a half-way house all took the Silva course. Six months later, twelve had not had another drink! One had a few drinks and stopped on his own. Another drank for a couple of days and then stopped. Only one needed intervention to help him stop. That's considered a tremendous success rate for hard-core alcoholics.

Do what they did: Use your level—the powerful alpha levels—to provide you with a choice: to drink or not to drink.

Create New Habits to Help You Succeed

You may feel a bit apprehensive when you start practicing any techniques to help you become more successful. That just shows that you have a good fight-or-flight mechanism. As long as the techniques are new, as long as they represent something you are not accustomed to, you might notice this slight apprehension.

That's all right. Simply accept that as part of the growth process. It is a sign that you are doing it correctly.

Overcoming that feeling is very simple:

Keep practicing.

Make up your mind to keep on practicing the new behavior

until you become accustomed to it. Once you are used to it, it will seem more natural to do it than not.

In other words, you will have developed a habit—a success habit.

If you have developed the habit of brushing your teeth every night, and then one night you get in late and get in bed without brushing your teeth, you will probably feel uncomfortable as a result, perhaps so much so that you will get up and brush your teeth and then go back to bed.

The same thing happens when you get into the habit of entering your level every morning, or of making a list every night of tasks you need to do the next day. Skip one of these activities, and you will feel uncomfortable. That is, after you have done it enough to make it a habit.

How long does it take to create a good habit? Not long at all. In fact, ten days should be plenty of time. That is one reason we ask you to practice a technique for ten days—to make a habit of it.

Remember, you only use force in the physical dimension. When using mental techniques, the strategy is not confrontation, but cooperation. Relax, and use your greatest asset: your mind. Reflect on what you want, especially at level. Keep your thoughts positive by thinking only about what you want. This will attract exactly what you desire. In the mental dimension, you do not use effort. You do use imagination.

Imitate a Superstar

Navigating the road to success is easy when you have a map. You can follow in the footsteps of those who have gone before you, and then go on beyond.

Create your own success habits by finding someone you consider very successful and imitate their habits. They have already blazed a trail to success. Follow their trail, then use your own talents and energies to go beyond it.

You might find them getting up earlier and working later than the losers. You will find that they are well organized.

Notice also the "people skills" they possess, and let this guide you to making your own habits.

You can't be another person. You are unique, you are yourself. But when you see habits that are common to successful people, then it makes sense for you to create similar habits in your own life.

Look for the Good and Praise It

One final thought before we finish this chapter: Recognize feedback for what it is. If your task is getting easier, you are going in the right direction.

Remember Christopher Columbus? He was sailing west, searching for fame and fortune. His goal was a continent with untold riches. He sailed on faith, and somehow managed to keep his crew under control.

But his first sighting was not of a continent. First he saw some branches, some twigs, floating in the water.

Did he think that he had failed when his goal was a continent but all he found were twigs?

Far from it. He viewed the twigs as a sign of progress. If tree branches were floating in the water, could land be far away? The discovery empowered him, gave him renewed faith and energy.

Remember when you are working on your projects, as long as you are making progress, you are moving in the correct direction.

Keep going. Never give up. You cannot fail . . . unless you quit. If you are not getting positive feedback, then adjust your direction. But always keep going.

We remember Christopher Columbus because he kept going until he reached his goal. Set your goals, make your plans, then keep going.

Limiting Belief Systems

Reality is anything that solves problems.
If we cannot see it, but it solves problems, then it is real.

—José Silva

Can your thoughts affect your physical body?

Sure they can. To see how your thoughts can affect your body, do the following exercise. (You will need a friend to help you.)

1. Hold one arm out straight to your side, parallel to the floor, hand open, thumb pointing down. Have your friend test your strength by pushing your arm down while you resist. (If you are too strong for your friend, then test your strength by forming a circle with the thumb and first finger of either of your hands, holding them tightly together and seeing if your friend can pull them apart.)

2. Now relax for a moment. When you are ready, hold your arm out again in the same position, but this time think about something that makes you sad, perhaps sometime

when you failed to accomplish what you needed to. While holding this thought, have your friend test your strength again. This time your friend will find it much easier to push your arm down.

3. Relax again. Then think about your most recent success, a very satisfying success, one that you are proud of. Once again, have your friend test your strength. You will be much stronger when thinking about success.

Have your friend test your strength as you think about different experiences of when you failed or succeeded. Think about people who encourage you and people who criticize you and make fun of you. You will find that when you are confident, you are strong; when you have doubts, you are weak.

Mind guides brain and brain guides body, so your mind definitely controls your body by directing and regulating the neurotransmitters in your brain.

How Our Beliefs Are Formed

We all have beliefs lurking inside of us that inhibit us from achieving all that we can achieve. But these beliefs are usually hidden from us, because we accept them as being reality instead of just beliefs about reality.

The information that we take in during the first few years of life influences everything we do for the rest of our lives.

During the first seven years of life, your brain functions inductively. You have not yet developed critical consciousness, the ability to analyze information and accept what is good for you and reject what is not.

By the time your brain matures enough so that it can function deductively, you have already learned most of what you are going to learn in your lifetime.

Most of this information is buried in the subconscious. The average person does not have access to this information, and that is why it is called subconscious.

José Silva found a way to convert the subconscious into an inner conscious level, so that you can go in and rewire the circuits, so to speak. You can neutralize negative past programs, and install new programs into the biocomputer that is your brain, programs that can override the original programs that were installed when you were too young to analyze them or make informed decisions about them.

Almost every parent, in an attempt to motivate their child, has said: "Make good grades if you want to be successful in life." Most of us were told that, and we formed an association between the grades we made and how successful we will be in life.

The truth is that only a few people make the highest grades, a few make the lowest, and most of us are in the middle. We are average.

If our belief system is that our successes in life is linked to the grades we made in school, then we will be predisposed to be average in life.

How difficult is it to neutralize the belief systems that might be holding you back and replace them with beneficial beliefs? Very difficult—at the beta, outer conscious level.

Such changes are well within reach at the alpha, inner conscious level. All it takes is a plan and persistence.

Change Personality Traits

Psychometric tests reveal your attitudes, and how you tend to react to various situations. If you change the programs in your biocomputer—your brain—then these changes will show up on the psychometric tests.

You can use the Silva techniques to make such changes, and you can verify them by testing.

You've heard that some people are born salesmen, while others couldn't sell a drink of water in the desert!

Much of this is due to the personality that we develop as we are growing up.

Is there any way that a person can change their basic personality?

Is there any way that José Silva's System can help?

You bet!

That's exactly what happened with Ed Bernd Jr. Here he is. explaining in his own words how he went from being a person who would back down in a confrontation to someone whose persuasive skills were above average, according to a test of personality traits.

From "Extremely Mild Ego Drive" to "Above Average" Leadership Potential

Back when I first started teaching the Silva course, I realized that I did not have good selling skills. As a result, few people were attending my seminars.

So I applied for a job as a newspaper advertising salesperson, in order to have an opportunity to learn some sales skills. I grew up in the newspaper business, so I figured this should be a relatively easy product for me to sell.

The advertising director of the newspaper had me take a personality test, one that took three hours to complete!

When he read the results to me over the phone a few days later, I began to learn a lot about myself.

First, there were a lot of good things:

"Really intelligent; very, very bright." Other good things followed, like "loving" and "very energetic" and "a good communicator (probably talks too much)." He paused, and I agreed: "No arguments so far."

But then came a comment, "Extremely mild ego drive, very unassertive. He'll avoid confrontation situations. If one occurs, he'll back down."

Again the advertising director paused, and again I agreed with the assessment. "Right on," I said.

Then there were several more good things, such as "Pays great attention to detail, social, creative."

And then came the verdict:

"Lacks in a major way the inner need to persuade people. Absolutely not a salesperson. I'm very puzzled why he applied for a sales position." They recommended me for a job in customer service.

Well, to look at it in a positive sense, I certainly had plenty of room for improvement, so I asked the advertising director if he would give me a copy of the evaluation. I told him that I planned to use the Silva techniques to make some changes. He was kind enough to give me a copy.

I went to work using the Silva techniques, and also taking action in the physical world. Good intentions are not enough; you have to put your plans into action if you want results.

A little over two years later, I took a test administered to Silva instructors by one of our researchers. He was looking for traits of good instructors, and this test measures sixteen personality factors.

The new test indicated that, in a group of peers, my potential for leadership is above average. This was the first time anybody ever said I had any leadership ability. It went on to say that potential for success in jobs that reward interpersonal, sales, and persuasive skills is above average. I'd come a long way from "very unassertive. He'll avoid confrontation."

I had gained many new, desirable, personal characteristics without losing any of the good traits I had before.

Identifying the Problem

I realized later, after many hours analyzing my situation at deep levels, that I had what Academy Award–winning actress Jane Fonda recently referred to as "a disease to please." It didn't help that I'd had polio at age five and wasn't as strong or as fast as the other kids. I was ridiculed and bullied a lot, and had few friends growing up. The daily beatings from my mother didn't help either.

In my humble opinion, spanking is not a good way to correct bad behavior. The pain is so intense that it takes attention away from the behavior you are trying to change. There are better ways of creating consequences that relate directly to the "bad" behavior. I have gone through my life terrified that if I offend or displease somebody in any way, they might hurt me. Of course I wouldn't speak up for myself, and I would back down in a confrontation.

People sensed that in me too. For a long time I wondered why I had so much trouble persuading people to take the Silva course with me. Now I understand: why should they, when they sensed, at a deep level, that I didn't have enough confidence in myself and my own opinions to stand up for myself?

Early Experiences Can Have Long-Term Effects

Childhood abuse can bring about feelings of shame and unworthiness that affect us for the rest of our lives. Some people are fortunate enough to overcome them, while others never do.

Jane Fonda spoke out recently about being raped and sexually abused as a child, saying she was raised with "the disease to please" other people. She said it took her sixty years to "learn how to say no."

Legendary blues singer Peggy Lee wrote about the daily whippings her stepmother administered through her teenage years in a song titled "One Beating a Day."

Lee wrote in her memoirs that her stepmother "hit me over the head with a cast-iron skillet [and] beat me with a heavy leather razor strap with a metal end." The beatings left a scar on one side of her face, which Lee had to cover with makeup before appearing publicly.

"I think it took her a long time to get over and deal with that part of her life," Lee's daughter Foster said. "But once she was able to put it behind her, she was even able to joke about it. And of course, there's very little humor in something like that." (The quote comes from a *Los Angeles Times* article from January 23, 2002, announcing the singer's death.)

Author and activist Stacey Patton PhD says that "we've got fifty years' worth of science that has shown that hitting children causes structural damage to their brains. It sparks biochemical responses that can put a child at risk for a lowered IQ, depression, alcohol abuse, delinquency and even chronic health problems like diabetes, heart issues, cancer and even a lowered life span," she said.

Some people "are successful in spite of having had somebody assault their bodies as children," Patton continued. Some of them "are people who are victims of unrecognized trauma," she added. You can read more in her book *Spare the Kids* and on her website: www.sparethekids.com.

Joe Girard, author of several best-selling books including *How to Sell Anything to Anybody*, is one person who overcame severe abuse to become successful. He has written about how his father used to tie him up in the basement and beat him with a belt while telling him how worthless he was. Girard wrote that for years he failed at everything he tried, even at being a petty thief.

Then one day he persuaded an auto dealer to hire him as a salesman. He was desperate because he needed to buy groceries for his wife and baby. That night, he wrote, he sold his first car. He said he could still recall the details of the sale except what the customer looked like. When he looked at the customer, all he saw was the bag of groceries he needed.

For the next twelve years Girard sold more new retail cars and trucks than any other salesperson. This got him listed in the *Guinness Book of World Records* as the number one automobile and truck salesperson in the world.

Creative people like Jane Fonda and Peggy Lee tend to function a lot in the alpha level, and their careers tend to keep them focused on their goal. The memories of the pain that they had suffered is something they could use to put more power into their performances.

The kind of desperation that Joe Girard felt when he was trying to sell that car can activate and mobilize all parts of your brain.

When Girard looked at the customer and only saw a bag of groceries, he was doing what we have been talking about: leap-frogging over the problem and concentrating on the solution. He was also thinking about how this would benefit someone else, not himself.

Girard recognizes the value of the Silva System. He said that it will help to "make you become the World's Greatest Anything."

You now have more tools and better tools to work with than they had: you have a scientifically researched and proven System that allows you to function at the inner conscious level and apply proven techniques to neutralize old, negative past programming and limiting beliefs, and create beneficial solutions in all areas of your business and personal life.

In this book, you have already learned how to enter the powerful alpha level and function there with conscious awareness so you can analyze problems and create solutions. You now have it within your power to neutralize any negative programming and limiting beliefs that reside in your "subconscious" and achieve the success you desire. I know because I did it.

Here is how I did it:

Three Steps to Success

What did I do to accomplish such a personality change in just over two years?

Three broad steps were involved:

1. I became aware of the problem. At the alpha level, I was guided to seek help in sales. That's why I answered the classified ad seeking a sales representative.

   The test that I took gave me valuable insight. I spent a couple of hours with a dictionary, studying the definitions of the words *convince* and *persuade*. I realized that I was very good at convincing people that the Silva course was very valuable and could help them, but I wouldn't even attempt to persuade them to take the course. If they wanted to attend, fine. If not, too bad. Obviously, I wasn't making many sales or helping many people.

   Once I understood the problem, I moved on to the solution, represented by the next two steps:

2. I did a lot of programming. Here are some of the techniques I used:

   Visualization and imagination with the Three-Scenes Technique to mentally picture myself persuading people to attend the course.

   Mental Rehearsal, which makes it even easier to get your feelings involved. I imagined the feelings I'd have when I persuaded someone to register, knowing how much they would benefit, and that it was because of my persistence and persuasiveness that they would ultimately enjoy those benefits.

   I did a lot of creative thinking at my level. One of the Silva instructors that I had consulted with suggested that I use my "pretend" technique, where I would simply pretend to have the traits that I desired. (Ed described his pretending technique in chapter 5.)

I rehearsed all of these things at my level many, many times. I rehearsed them mentally before I ever tried them. After every sales presentation, I'd enter my level and review what I had done, and use the Three-Scenes Technique to correct any mistakes, to say the things I had forgotten to say, to correct my tone of voice and my posture.

And I'd reinforce my successes. I'd recall and review that special feeling of success that you get when everything goes right. I'd relive those moments over and over again at my level, knowing that every time I reviewed the success and the special feeling of success, I would benefit. With every sale I made in the physical world, I got as much experience as if I'd made a hundred sales, because I'd make it over and over again at the alpha level.

As you may have noticed, I did much more than imagine selling. And that's the final step: Go do it.

3. I took action in the physical world.

One of the first things I did was to purchase a book on assertiveness training and study it. In the book, I realized that there is a difference between *assertive* and *aggressive.* I enjoy being assertive—standing up for what I believe in. I don't like being aggressive.

So I looked for every possible opportunity to practice being assertive and persuasive.

I found an easy place to practice: the local flea market.

At the flea market, no matter how much I wanted something, no matter that it was worth more to me than they were asking for it, I simply refused to buy anything unless I could persuade the seller to reduce the price, or throw in an additional item. I walked away from things I really wanted rather than give in.

The Silva Systems provided me with the techniques that I could use to make beneficial changes in my personality.

You can do the same. Use your level to determine what you need to do. Perhaps you will use some of the same techniques and strategies that I used, or perhaps you will come up with even better ideas at your level—the alpha level.

You saw in the demonstration at the beginning of this chapter how your thoughts can affect your body and sap your strength, or give you more strength.

In the section below, José Silva will tell us in his own words how your thoughts can make you ill—the "psychosomatic effect"— and how your thoughts can make you well and keep you healthy.

Use the Psychosomatic Effect to Keep You Well

The undisciplined mind can make you sick.

It is generally agreed in the medical profession that as many as 90 percent of health problems, or even more, are psychosomatic.

Psychosomatic means that the mind (the psyche) influences the body (the *soma*), causing a health problem.

It all starts with fear. Fear is always interpreted by the body as a threat to life. Worrying about anything is a form of fear.

Fear causes the autonomic nervous system to prepare the body for fight or flight. There is wear and tear on the body from adjusting to the fight-or-flight condition.

Wear and tear causes stress, and stress weakens the body's immune system. It is then that health problems begin.

In order to correct this condition, we must learn to place our mind in neutral. When the mind is in neutral, it frees the immune system to do its job, and that is to keep the body healthy by normalizing the abnormal.

Doctors and medicines do not heal; they help the body to heal itself.

For some health problems, the mind needs to be placed in neutral once a day for fifteen minutes.

For other health problems, the mind needs to be placed in neutral two or even three times a day, for fifteen minutes each time.

Learning to place your mind in neutral helps your doctor accelerate the healing process.

Worry triggers the fight-or-flight response, activating the body's survival mechanism and causing stress, which in turn causes wear and tear on the body, and the wear and tear causes even more stress.

The autonomic nervous system (the body's survival mechanism) is composed of: the sympathetic nervous system, which accelerates the function of glands, organs, and organ systems; and the parasympathetic nervous system, which decelerates the function of glands, organs, and organ systems.

The autonomic nervous system should function according to the body's needs, but false fear sends false signals and can cause a gland, organ, or organ system to overwork. This results in stress, weakening the immune system, and eventually results in a gland, organ, or organ system breakdown. This causes more stress, and the cycle continues getting worse and worse.

In lay terms, when worry or fear activates the fight-or-flight response, your heart beats faster, your muscles get tense, and your whole system starts working overtime.

When you put your mind in neutral at alpha, you cannot worry. This allows your parasympathetic nervous system to decelerate the function of your glands, organs, and organ systems, and function only according to the body's real needs.

Some people develop a habit of wrong thinking that eventually develops into what is called a disease.

A chronic health condition can be the cause of a fixed pattern of thinking, holding onto false concepts. This condition causes the glands to deposit the chemicals that cause the health problem into the circulatory system.

When the mind does not interfere with the functioning of the human body, the body knows naturally how to heal itself.

You will accelerate the healing process when you are able to place your mind in neutral from time to time and combine this with any medication that your doctor has prescribed for you.

Correcting from the Inner to the Outer

In this field of science we correct problems from the inner to the outer levels of matter. Objective medicine is from the outer to the inner levels of matter.

We come from within, working outwards. Objective medicine comes from outwards, working within.

So we are at the very root, where things do happen. They can be corrected more easily than from the outer levels.

So we want to know, where do we meet, medicine and our thing? Is it more physical than psychological, or is it more psychological than physical?

Research indicates that 99.99 percent of the problems are partly in one and partly in the other. They are not all psychological; they are not all biological.

What percentage is psychological, and what percentage is biological? It varies.

So remember that we work from the inner to the outer, with our minds. Objective medicine works from the outer to the inner.

For health we know that we can accelerate healing, control psychosomatic health problems, and convert the polarity of the health problems into a positive, constructive, creative, thing instead of a negative, detrimental thing.

The mind can help the body heal itself.

She Used Her Mind to Straighten Her Spine

A young woman named Tracy Kay Huddleston of Puyallup, Washington used the Silva techniques to deal with scoliosis: curvature of the spine. She told us:

At first I was doing various physical exercises my father found by researching. These exercises were helpful to a degree, as they aligned my hips and lower back; however, my upper back was still out of alignment and was not getting any better.

I stopped doing the exercises and instead began using Silva techniques to visualize my spine straight and myself standing tall. Sometimes I would imagine "pushing" my spine into place with my hands, or some kind of healing light shining upon my spine to make it properly aligned.

I usually did this at least once or twice a day and found it made a big difference in just a matter of days. After a few weeks, the curve in my spine is now almost entirely unnoticeable.

Before I started treating it, a DO (doctor of osteopathic medicine) stated it was so bad that surgery was the only fix for it, so I feel like this is a major accomplishment. Although the exercises helped with half of the scoliosis, I feel as though using the Silva techniques could've been enough to heal all of it had I started using it at the very beginning. I'm very impressed with the results.

I was pretty confident the Silva exercises would work, and listening to other people's success was helpful with confidence for sure. Using Silva on a frequent basis was helpful too, because every success, no matter how small, gave a boost in my confidence in the techniques.

Part Three

Guiding Principles

Guidance from Higher Intelligence

We don't knock down doors. If it opens, OK.
If not, look for another door.

—José Silva

At some point you have probably wondered:

Why am I here? Does my life have some meaning, some purpose?

When José Silva meditated on that question, the answer that came to him is that we were sent here to correct problems, to complete the creation of the planet, and convert the planet into a paradise.

He always tested the ideas and theories that came to him by asking if they are practical: can they be used to solve problems in the real world?

The idea that we should try to solve as many problems as possible is very practical: the more problems we can work on, the better we get at solving problems—including our own.

That is not the only reason that we should try to solve problems. We are all part of something much greater than just our individual selves.

The Sum Is Greater than the Parts

Humanity is like a team; life is like team support. Some individuals have more talent than others, and some get more recognition and rewards than others, but ultimately, we all win or lose together as a team.

It doesn't stop there.

As his thinking continued to evolved, Mr. Silva began to realize that we are more than a part of humanity. He realized that humanity itself is part of something far greater:

We are a vital part of hierarchy of intelligences that he refers to as *higher intelligence.* Higher intelligence is his term for what some people call God, or Allah, or the Almighty, or Jehovah, or some other name.

We All Have a Part to Play

"If we use common sense," Mr. Silva said, "it does not make sense that only one entity should take care of the whole universe, because if so, then why did this one entity, the entity that some people call God, need us to do something on planet earth?

"If God could have done it by himself, then we would not be needed.

"We were created by a power known as God to take care of the needs of the planet, because God is busy doing other things."

He compared the hierarchy of intelligences that he calls *higher intelligence* to the systems that we set up on planet earth to take care of business.

When you want to buy a new car, for instance, you don't go to the president of General Motors. You go to your local dealership. If you have a problem with your new car, you take it to the dealership and they assign a mechanic to fix the problem. If they cannot fix the problem, then they go higher up to find someone who can. When it is repaired, you say, "General Motors took care of my problem."

We organize government the same way.

If a streetlight on your street burns out, you don't need to call the mayor to fix it; you call the public works department. Then you say, "The city replaced my street light."

Mr. Silva said that when we create this type of hierarchy, we are copying the hierarchy of intelligences that governs the universe.

The Way We Can Help Higher Intelligence

God is not physical, God is spiritual. God doesn't have physical senses to detect what is happening on planet earth; God doesn't have a physical body to correct problems in the physical dimension.

That is why we are necessary.

It is through us, who were created in the image of God, that God can be present here on earth.

You could say that we are like the public works department we mentioned a moment ago: we are the ones assigned to go and fix the problem.

We use our physical senses to see what is going on here on planet earth, then we use visualization—mental images—to send information back to "headquarters," to higher intelligence on the other side.

Then higher intelligence—in the spiritual dimension—will guide us and help us by providing "coincidences" in the physical world that we can *see* with our physical eyes.

We don't have to guess what to do. We can see what to do when we see the coincidences, the indications that we get from higher intelligence.

"Coincidences," Mr. Silva said, "are God's way of showing his hand."

How to Ask for Guidance and Help

It is very easy to ask for help, provided that the help you are asking for will improve conditions on planet earth, and will benefit more than just one person.

You can learn the MentalVideo technique right now and use it tonight to ask for the help you need.

The MentalVideo is a scientifically based, reliable, and verifiable way to pray. You will notice that it uses José Silva's concept of higher intelligence and the tutor, which we will present below in the section entitled "Who Is Listening to Us on the Other Side?" But first, here is the formula for the MentalVideo technique itself:

The MentalVideo Technique

Here is what you do before going to bed:

1. At beta with eyes open, mentally create, with visualization, a MentalVideo of a problem.
2. Include everything that belongs to the animate matter kingdom. Animate matter means everything that contains life. The MentalVideo must include everything animate that concerns the problem.
3. After having completed the MentalVideo of the problem, use visualization to review it at beta, with your eyes closed.

Here is what to do when you are in bed and ready to go to sleep. You might want to sit up in bed while doing this so that you don't fall asleep before you complete all five steps:

1. To use the MentalVideo Technique, enter your level with the 3 to 1 Method when you are in bed and ready to go to sleep. Once you are at your level, review the MentalVideo that you created of the problem at beta.
2. After you have reviewed the problem, mentally convert the problem into a project. Then create, with imagination, a MentalVideo of the solution.
3. The MentalVideo of the solution should contain a step-by-step procedure of how you desire the project to be resolved.
4. After both of the MentalVideos have been completed, go to sleep with the intention of delivering the MentalVideo to your tutor while you sleep. Take for granted that the delivery will be made.
5. During the next three days, look for indications that point to the solution. Every time you think of the project, think

of the solution that you created in the MentalVideo, in a past tense sense.

When Learning, Do Exactly What the Formula Says

Anytime you are learning something new, it is best to learn it exactly the way you are taught, and not try to modify the procedure. Once you have had some success with a technique, then you have a baseline that you can use to see if your modifications help or not.

José Silva spent a lot of time considering every word he used in his formulas. He had at least three dictionaries on his desk, both English and Spanish. You can rely on what he wrote.

For instance, in Step 5, when he says to "*look* for indications that point to the solution," he means to use your physical eyes. The Merriam-Webster dictionary defines "look" this way: "to ascertain by the use of one's eyes."

In order to be scientifically valid, we need objective verification and replication. In other words: physical-world results that you can see, and the ability to confirm them.

Suppose you have a flash of insight that seems to contain a solution to the problem. In that case, act on it and look at the results. If your insight was only your own fantasy, then it will not solve the problem. On the other hand, if you act on it and make progress towards solving the problem, then you can assume that it was guidance from higher intelligence.

When Mr. Silva says to mentally convert the problem into a project, he means to create a solution in the mental dimension. Thought always precedes action. The solution is created first in the subjective (mental) dimension, and therefore there is no more problem—in the subjective dimension. While we are working on it in the physical world, we know it is already done in the mental world, so we refer to it as a "project."

Who Is Listening to Us on the Other Side?

The tutor is an entity in the spiritual dimension that has been assigned to help us. Some people compare it to a guardian angel.

Mr. Silva sometimes compared his concept of higher intelligence to the situation of astronauts on the moon. If you have seen the movie about the Apollo 13 spacecraft, which was severely damaged on the way to the moon, you probably recall the famous line: "Houston, we have a problem."

The astronauts were calling on a "higher power" for help to solve a critical, life-threatening problem that was too big for them to solve alone.

When they said, "Houston . . . " they weren't referring to the city of Houston, Texas. They weren't referring to the director of NASA. They were actually communicating with the person who had been designated the Capsule Communicator, or Capcom.

The Capsule Communicator in turn went to the appropriate engineers and asked them to get to work on the problem. The engineers reported back to the Capcom, and he relayed the information to the astronauts aboard the damaged spacecraft.

José Silva's research—along with the successes we've observed when people use the MentalVideo Technique—confirms that our relationship to God is much the same. When we pray, we ask for help from God, and the request is heard by the one entity that has been assigned to communicate with us—our tutor.

Advice from a Natural Alpha Thinker

We found an author whose ideas seemed to be very much like José Silva's. The author is Robert Collier, and many of his books are still available from his family.

We found a paragraph in Collier's book *Riches within Your Reach: The Law of the Higher Potential*, published in 1947, just three years before his death, that answers a question that many Silva grads have asked during the years: "Why is it when I have a really strong desire for something, and I really need it, and it will benefit many people, and I program really hard for it, I still don't get results? I get great results on little things that are not so important; why not this?"

Collier's guidance also expresses one of the main principles that José Silva incorporated into the UltraMind Systems—we do all that we can to fulfill the plan that higher intelligence has for us. Here is the way Robert Collier said it in his book *Riches Within Your Reach, the Law of the Higher Potential* published in 1947 by Robert Collier Publications

Look at the first chapter of the Scriptures. When God wanted light, did He strive and struggle, trying to make light? No, He said—"Let there be light."

When you want something very much, instead of trying to *make* it come your way, suppose you try asking for it and then *letting* it come. Suppose you just relax, and let God work through you instead of trying to make Him do something for you. Suppose you say to yourself—"I will do whatever is given me to do. I will follow every lead to the best of my ability, but for the rest, it is all up to the God in me. God in me knows what my right work is, where it is, and just what I should do to get it.

I put myself and my affairs lovingly in His hands, secure that whatever is for my highest good, He will bring to me."

José Silva said we were sent here for a purpose, with a job to do. If we fulfill that purpose, then we will be happy, fulfilled, and prosperous. Now you know how to program to fulfill your mission successfully.

The MentalVideo in Action

Here are some stories of the MentalVideo in action. The first one shows how you might get something even better than what you ask for if you leave room for guidance from higher intelligence.

That is what happened to Maria T. Caro of Stockton, California. Here is her story in her own words:

I would love to share my success story to inspire others, so here it goes:

I had three job interviews lined up for a sales position, all where I planned to relocate in the Tri-Valley area in California.

The first one was my top choice. I was really so excited and wanted to get this job so badly that I called Katherine Sandusky to guide me and make sure I do the right thing in pursuing this position. Kathy patiently helped me out to program with the MentalVideo and advised me to ask for indications.

I went to this interview, and during the interview I knew immediately that this may not be the right one for me. So even though I was not offered the position, I had moved on to two other interviews, one in the morning and the other one in the afternoon.

I included these in the MentalVideo technique. I kept in mind what I wanted—with the images of the exact kind of people and company I'll be working with, the exact compensation, the city where I want to work and live.

During my interviews on both, I knew and felt I got the positions. Both offered me the position on the same day of interview.

I had to choose which one I should accept. After considering all options (things I asked for), I accepted the third company, which was so excited to get me on board. They offered me base salary plus commission, an excellent benefit package, and I will be a key sales specialist with this international company, with amazing staff and definitely so much room for advancement. It's also in the city I wanted—Pleasanton, California.

I also programmed to get a place as close as possible to my work, and I got a place just one highway exit away from it. It is so close that I can walk to my work if I want to. I feel blessed.

I thank Kathy for helping and guiding me during this process. I believe everything is that is possible is within your reach as long as you know what you want, and then watch for indications. Things will happen that will benefit all everybody concerned. Good luck to everyone!

Duty-Bound to Serve Humanity Better

It is much easier to be enthusiastic and positive and persuasive when you are doing your right work, especially when your work is helping people to change their lives for the better.

Chen Bin of Tianjin, China, used the MentalVideo to help her find her right work. It began when Xue Kuiyang, the Silva

UltraMind Systems director in China, called and suggested that she become an UltraMind ESP Systems instructor.

> I was stressed at that time, because I was not confident on one hand, and I had to independently conduct the course. But meanwhile I still believed that there was a better arrangement. [So she used the MentalVideo technique.]
>
> In the problem video, I visualized receiving the call from my instructor, Xue Kuiyang, inviting me to teach the first Silva UltraMind ESP System course independently. I felt happy but nervous.
>
> Though I believed this would be a new stage to accomplish my life mission, and was grateful for my instructor Xue Kuiyang's trust, I was bewildered how to do it well. I asked higher intelligence to guide me and let me know clearly what to do and how to proceed.
>
> In the solution video, I imagined that I got the guidance from higher intelligence in a timely manner, that I correctly understood the guidance, and prepared the sixty-first course step by step.
>
> I also imagined that when the course was over, I had a dinner with my assistant and celebrated the success of the course. Those who benefited from the course were me and all those who benefited from accomplishment of my life mission, and I was improved too. I also expressed my gratitude to higher intelligence, Mr. José Silva, and Xue Kuiyang.
>
> On the second day after sending out my mental videos, I entered the alpha level and turned on my Mental Screen. A clear schedule that fit me well came out, and I confirmed objectively that the schedule would work. Then my mind became calm.

What to Do When Fear Confronts Your Desire to Succeed

Then a new problem came out. Every time I got up to teach the course, I had a serious cough. I tried many ways to stop it, but didn't help.

Then I used the Mental Screen to communicate with José Silva.

I told him my problem. He smiled and told me, "I chose you. Don't worry. You are duty-bound." Immediately I became calm again. Since I was chosen by José Silva, from the spiritual dimension, I believed that José Silva and Xue Kuiyang were with me all the time. Now I needed to communicate with my body to build up my confidence.

I entered the alpha level and mentally projected myself onto the Mental Screen. I asked my body why it reacted with a cough. Then a black microwave oven appeared, with yellow sparks in it. I asked what it meant.

There came some words: "What you want and what you are afraid of met each other." Then I asked how to solve the problem. The answer was to turn off the power and relax.

Gradually my cough got better, and I am fine now.

From the beginning of this experience to end, everything turned out well. The whole time, I believed higher intelligence was offering me the best guidance because this is my life duty. Now my stress has turned into duty. I am quite calm now when I teach the Silva courses.

This was confirmed again when the first day of the class over. One participant came over to me and bowed to me to thank me. My eyes turned wet. I was touched. In this Silva course, the instructor and participant grew together.

How Higher Intelligence Can Help You
with a Worthwhile Project

Xue Kuiyang, the Silva UltraMind director in China, used the MentalVideo in another way: to help her with a project that was very important to her. The following is how the project came together, in her own words:

The end of 2015 completed ten years of the Silva UltraMind ESP System and José Silva's Holistic Faith Healing System in China. The systems were now firmly established in China in accordance with Chinese philosophy, culture, and medicine.

I planned to hold a celebration in 2016 to celebrate your success with UltraMind and to announce the birth of two new programs I have developed to further José Silva's work: Cyberbradionet-Brain and Xue's Taiji Zen System.

I prepared the conference notice, but felt that the notice was not ideal except for its time and place. I still needed to develop its format, its theme, its contents, its benefits, its fee collection, and its invited guests and number of participants.

I wasn't sure what to do, and I wanted it to be very special, so I decided to use the MentalVideo to ask for guidance and help from higher intelligence. A series of "coincidences" followed, which brought me much more than I had imagined.

On the second day after using the MentalVideo technique, the idea came to me that 2016 was also the fiftieth anniversary of Silva's courses being opened to the public; and coincidently, it was also my fiftieth birthday year. I was born nearly the same day as when the Silva Mind Control course was first taught to the public. This inspired me to work even harder on this project.

I contacted UltraMind headquarters in the United States and asked them to send me a greeting letter to the event, or even a video greeting if they could. This inspired Ed Bernd to put together a video of the multi-image slide show he presented at the 1989 international Silva convention in Laredo, Texas. It including dozens of pictures of Laredo, the Silva offices, the Silva family home, and a celebration of Mother's Day at the Silva ranch. Ed said he had wanted to do this for years, and now it can be viewed by everyone on the YouTube website: www.youtube.com/watch?v=BBd2hCNqXBM.

The plans began to come together quickly after that:

Li Hong, one of our Silva graduates, got her friend to help us with the format of the notice announcing the conference.

Chen Bin, one of the Silva UltraMind ESP System instructors in China, arranged for Li Ming, a doctor of psychology who specializes in oriental psychology, to be our academic advisor and give the keynote address, including his evaluation of Silva UltraMind Systems and our new Cyberbradionet-Brain and Xue's Taiji Zen System.

An idea came to me to ignite candles for Silva graduates at the event. Coincidentally, Katherine Sandusky sent me a photo of José Silva doing the same for Silva graduates at one of the annual conventions in Laredo.

The guidance I received with the help of the MentalVideo led me to make several changes to my original plans:

At the beginning, the event was more about "me" and the "2016 annual conference."

Later on I got the guidance about how all participants could benefit the most. I asked all participants to give a short introduction and a brief presentation about themselves and their institutions so that the Silva UltraMind Institute of China Ltd. could be positioned as a platform for all Chinese Silva graduates to be mission-oriented. Many institutions reached strategy agreement with the Silva UltraMind Institute of China Ltd. for future cooperation.

Silva graduate Chen Ping's company presented some gifts for all participants of the event. Another company arranged a test of fingerprints for participants to learn objectively and scientifically about their inborn potentials and how to unlock them easily.

There was one coincidence at the conference itself that confirmed to me that we had understood the guidance and done everything correctly: One of our Silva graduates presented me a beautiful colorful paper-cut painting with a vibrant horse. I was born in 1966, the Year of the Horse.

In the end, there were far more benefits to many more people than I had imagined in the beginning, thanks to the guidance I received from higher intelligence when I used the MentalVideo technique.

It is really wonderful to have a heaven-human partnership as one lifestyle, as our Chinese cultural term says. It is what José Silva calls the beginning of second phase of the second phase of human evolution on the planet. Every day we are daydreaming and night-dreaming, and we are realizing a better world day by day.

10

The Laws of Programming

*How much help you get from higher intelligence depends on
how big your plans are. The bigger your plans are—meaning . . .
how many people will benefit—the more help you will qualify for.*

—José Silva

José Silva learned at a very early age—just six years old—that the
more people he helped, the more money he made.

He learned that if he'd shine their shoes, they'd pay him. The
more shoes he shined, the more money he made. The better job he
did, the more repeat business he got.

Then one day he asked his uncle, who was helping him, why
so many men were looking at those big sheets of paper. His uncle
explained that they were reading the news, to learn what was
going on in town. So José found out where to get newspapers, and
offered them for sale to his customers.

And he made more money by doing that.

When he overheard some men talking about how difficult it
was to find an honest, reliable person to come in at night and
clean their offices, young José offered to do it. He was so enthusi-

astic about it that they decided to give him a chance. They tested him by leaving some money and a watch lying on a desk. José put them away, and the next day came and showed the men where he had put the money and watch. So they knew that they could trust him, and they saw that he would do a good job, and José made more money.

It's just logical: the more people you serve, the more service you provide, the more problems you solve, the more rewards you will receive.

There's no better proof of that than the Silva System itself. The more people José Silva helped with what he was learning in his research, the more he learned. It is as though the other side was giving him more information as they confirmed that he was using it, not for selfish purposes, but to correct problems. He never accepted any money for what he did; he was happy to do it.

And he was rewarded. The other side found a way to get $10,000 to him one time in the early 1950s to let him know that he should continue his research. That happened when he dreamed about some numbers one night, and they turned out to be for a winning lottery ticket. That was the only lottery ticket he ever bought.

Unfortunately, some people think that the Silva courses are just about getting things for yourself. It is sometimes marketed that way. But in the course, you learn that José Silva had something else in mind.

The first Beneficial Statement is: *my increasing mental faculties are for serving humanity better.*

You are advised that you mental faculties are increasing, and at the same time you are advised of what your obligations are.

As someone said a long time ago, "Much has been given to you, and much is expected of you."

How could a person not want to help someone who is hurting? How can anyone just walk away when they see somebody in need?

If you were not taught this when you were young, or if you have outgrown those natural instincts to help and to do constructive and creative things, then start working on getting to deep levels of mind. Get back to a level, to a time before you were contaminated, before fear and insecurity distorted your natural instincts and judgment.

That's what the Silva Centering Exercise does for us: It takes us back on the scale of brain evolution to an earlier age—brainwise—and reprograms us with these statements. It is almost like going back and changing your past. If you were not taught properly, now you can go back and do it right!

Beneficial Statements

We mentioned the Beneficial Statements in chapter 6 and discussed how they can help you heal the wounded child within. Here is some additional information about them and why they work so well. They have been part of the Silva courses since the very beginning more than fifty years ago:

> *My increasing mental faculties are for serving humanity better.*
> *Positive thoughts bring me benefits and advantages I desire.*
> *Every day in every way I am getting better, better, and better.*

Notice how each one leapfrogs over the task at hand—the current day's problems—and focuses on the solution:

The first statement doesn't talk about how to increase your mental faculties, but goes straight to the solution: serving humanity better.

Positive thinking is the problem; benefits and advantages are the solution.

The challenges of each day are helping to make me a better problem solver.

If you want to increase your mind power, you don't concentrate on increasing your mind power, because that is the problem you want to solve. Pushing to solve it is like pushing a strand of cooked spaghetti—you get a big wadded-up mess. You need to get out in front of the problem, leapfrog over it, and set your sights on the solution.

In every class we teach, there are people who wonder if they are "getting it." They don't know how to tell if they are actually getting to the alpha level or not, or if their mental faculties are actually increasing. That is normal.

So we imply that their mental faculties are increasing by asking them to repeat mentally: *My increasing mental faculties are for serving humanity better.*

José Silva focused on a solution, and he selected a solution with a lot of beneficiaries: *My increasing mental faculties are for serving humanity better.*

A man in one class heard that statement and asked: "But what about me?" Mr. Silva reminded him that he was part of humanity, and he would benefit along with everybody else.

Did you notice what the man *wasn't* thinking about? He wasn't questioning whether his mental faculties were increasing—whether he was gaining more mind power—only whether he was part of the group that would benefit from it.

All of the Beneficial Statements work the same way: they don't try to push their way through a problem, they get head of the problem and concentrate on a solution.

Laws of Programming

José Silva included something new in the Silva UltraMind ESP System. He called them the Laws of Programming. As their name suggests, these laws are to be considered when programming:

> *Do to others only what you like others to do to you.*
> *The solution must help to make this planet a better place to live.*
> *The solution must be the best for everybody concerned.*
> *The solution must help at least two or more persons.*
> *The solution must be within the possibility area.*

Laws are not optional: they are fixed, and they always apply. The law of gravity applies whether we believe in it or not. So do the Laws of Programming.

Some people ask if they can just program to get something for themselves, and we assure them that they can, but that they might not get any help from higher intelligence if they are asking *only* for themselves.

Remember that we are not alone on this planet. We occupy it along with other people, and whatever we do affects other people one way or another.

Let's say you want to get a new job that will pay you more money. Your first thought should be on what you can do that will be of more value. That is the lesson that José Silva learned when he was six years old.

Ask yourself: how many people will benefit from you working at the new job? Then, as Mr. Silva advised us, "Keep in mind what your needs are . . . plus a little bit more."

Will your family members benefit? Will you work harder and do more for your employer than most employees? Will this provide you with more opportunities and resources to help other people who need help?

Doing the work isn't the result of your getting paid. Just the opposite: getting paid is the result of the work that you do and the value you provide. The more people who benefit, the greater, the more valuable the work is. That's the only way to measure it: not by how hard we work, but by how many people benefit and how much value we provide.

The MentalVideo is not intended to help us get what we want, but to help us do what we were sent here to do. Mr. Silva said that we should spend every second of every day solving problems. Whenever you see a problem, he said, you should start thinking about what you might be able to do to correct it.

He took that to extremes sometimes. One day, as he left the office to go to lunch, he stood in the middle of the street, waving his hands and pointing to help the company's mechanic back a car out of the garage across the street. The mechanic did that numerous times every day and knew how to do it, but that didn't matter to José Silva: if he saw an opportunity to help, even in a small way, he did. He was a good role model.

Mr. Silva discovered that the people who experience the most success in all areas of life—not just financial, but health, relationships, happiness, sense of satisfaction, and so on—had a different attitude than the average person.

He continued to research and observe people, and this research—along with his own experience and the experiences of people who followed his guidance—convinced him that there is a certain attitude that is necessary if we are to be very successful.

As a result of all of his research and experience, he believed very strongly that we were sent here to planet earth to correct problems.

His advice has always been to program to provide service, and keep in mind what your needs are . . . plus a little bit more.

He said that we should be helping to convert the planet into a paradise.

When we develop these wonderful mental tools that we have, he felt that we should be using them to correct problems—without being concerned about whether we are compensated for this work or not.

Other people did a great deal of work so that we have what we have today. If José Silva had not worked for twenty-two years without ever accepting a penny for his efforts—we would not have the Silva Systems today.

From his research and experience for more than half a century, Mr. Silva felt that if we are only trying to help ourselves, then we are on our own, we are not going to get any help from higher intelligence.

But if we are working to correct the problems of humanity—because that is the right thing to do, because this is what we were sent here to do—then we will qualify for help from higher intelligence.

We know people who will do anything to help anyone . . . as long as there is something in it for them. That's barely adequate at best.

Anything that you program for should benefit at least two people, Mr. Silva said. That's the minimum; the more, the better.

The more problems you are solving—the more people you are helping—the more you qualify for help from higher intelligence. If you are just working for yourself, and doing things for yourself only, then you are not likely to get help from higher intelligence. You are on your own.

When you lift up humanity, you are also lifting yourself up, because you are a part of humanity.

Again, if you are only for yourself, then why should anyone else want to help you, or be associated with you? Would you want to do business with somebody who was only interested in how much he can get for himself? Would you want to marry a person who only wanted to get all they could from you?

If you are dedicated to helping humanity—without expecting to be directly compensated for it—then everyone will want to be associated with you, to do business with you, to be your friend.

At deep levels of mind, people seem to understand this without any problem. So if this seems like too strange a concept to you, go back to the Silva Centering Exercise, and practice deepening your level until you get back to the level before you were contaminated, to a time when things were more pure, clean, and positive.

In meditating on these ideas, Mr. Silva found a verse in the Bible that seemed to him to sum up the whole thing:

Seek ye first the kingdom of heaven, and function within God's righteousness, and all else will be added unto you.

The kingdom of heaven = the alpha state

God's righteousness = doing what God wants, on earth as it is in heaven

All else = everything you need, plus a little bit more

If you need a million dollars, he says, it is easy to get it: Just give ten million dollars' worth of service to humanity, and if you need a million dollars, you'll get it.

How José Silva Programmed for Money When He Needed It

Here is what José Silva wrote about programming for money:

> When programming for money, the first thing to think about is, what are you going to do when you get it?
>
> You don't want to just go away on a vacation and forget everything else. Your obligations still continue while you are still alive and still have the breath of life. Even if you have to drag yourself across the ground, you still have the same obligation to try and do your best to correct the problems on the planet. When you are not here anymore, then you cease to be obligated.
>
> If you do the right job, then money will come to you, because people who need you will request you, will ask for you, will attract you, and will be willing to pay you for your services.
>
> If you are a good worker, then everybody wants you, and will be willing to pay for your services. But if you're not, they don't want you.

This was why whenever I went to look for a job, when I was in the service and needed to supplement my income, everywhere I'd go they'd ask what I wanted to earn, and I answered, "Whatever you think I'm worth. Try me out, and pay me accordingly."

Prepare Yourself

All prosperity should be built on spiritual foundations. By *spiritual* we mean the functioning of mind, of human intelligence, in a nonphysical dimension.

Spiritual functioning means functioning in the subjective. That is where mind functions, where human intelligence functions, where desire functions, where belief and expectancy function, where love functions—all that is the spiritual dimension.

We need to first prepare that area and meet God's requirements, because in the spiritual dimension we cannot fool anybody.

Once we set our goals there, the next step will be to materialize them, to convert them or transfer them from one dimension to another. When we materialize them, then we are successful in having done so.

Use What You Create

Be successful first in the spiritual dimension. Then follow up on that success by taking advantage of what was conceived in the spiritual world, because what was conceived there will now manifest in the physical world. You help transfer it from one dimension to another.

That is the idea of the man who said, "Whatever the mind conceives in the spiritual dimension, and believes enough to transfer to the physical dimension, you will achieve." So the achievement was the transference of that particular thing that was created in the spiritual world into the material, physical world.

It is just like the materialization of thoughts. You have to first create them subjectively, in the mental world, and then you use them in the physical world, to make sense with them, to serve a purpose with them.

It is no good to just test them in one dimension. You have to go from one to another and have sense in both dimensions. The spiritual has to come first; we have to think about it before we act on it.

Do Your Thinking at Alpha

Thinking, planning, and analyzing are done in the mental world first; this is a requirement. This means the nonphysical. It means think about it—use your mind, your thoughts, your human intelligence.

In the mental dimension, you determine what you can do to improve living conditions on the planet. That is what we were sent here to do. Then you plan how to go about doing it. Then you transfer it to the physical dimension.

Plan it out, a step-by-step procedure. Establish short goals. Take the first step, followed by the second, and so forth.

Programming to Get Things

Suppose I want a new car. Here's how I would go about programming for it:

I wouldn't program for it just because I *want* it, but because I *need* it.

You may not always get what you want, but you can get what you need. Doing that depends on what you need it for. If it is to *cause* problems, you are not going to get it. If it is to *correct* problems, that's the reason you get it.

Again, remember the rules of the mental dimension: you have to think about it first, and set the rules mentally before they can be materialized.

You need to pass the test spiritually, meaning, is this correct? If it is, then you are going to get materially, physically, what you need.

Think about your goals first. Center yourself at 10 cycles of alpha brain-wave frequency, to be able to think correctly, because you could be off center, thinking eccentrically at the beta frequency of 20 cycles per second, which is no good. Centered thinking is what you want. Then most likely the right thoughts will come to you.

Center yourself by entering your level, the alpha level. Make sure that you have practiced and established points of reference so that you know when you are at alpha. You don't want to start daydreaming and let your mind wander and drift out of alpha.

You should justify your needs in all fairness. This is what I do in my business.

I program to attract whatever we need. I do not program to receive more than what we need, but I sure put emphasis on receiving *no less* than what we need.

Of course, you need to know in your own mind just what it is that you need. You don't have to ask for it, but keep it in mind, and everything will be automatic from there on.

You don't need to ask specifically for $50,000 if that's what you need; just keep your goal in mind, and program for all bills to be paid, or to have the things you need.

Program to see your projects completed, and keep in mind what it takes to do it, as though somebody were looking in and wanting to know what you need so they can send it your way, whatever your needs are. If you don't keep it in your mind, there is no way for them to know, whoever is trying to help you.

Use Your Possessions to Help Correct Problems

We don't plan to stack up millions and millions without using those millions, or at least letting somebody else use them.

Do you feel that everything you have acquired, you need? Or have you gotten some things you just want?

Everything that I have acquired, I think I have acquired it because I needed it.

Some people ask why I buy jewelry. Well, we don't have that much. It is to have a safety factor in case of an emergency. We don't want to cause problems for anybody. We don't want to go begging in case of an emergency. We can exchange it, so we can get whatever we need in an emergency. We don't have to bother somebody else.

I am not limiting you to just your physical needs. We could include psychological needs, emotional needs, social needs, and so forth. If it helps you work better, do a better job, then it is a need.

Help People to Help Themselves

Some people have questioned why I buy Cadillacs. They ask if it would be better to buy two Chevrolets, drive one myself, and give the other to a needy person who doesn't have a car but needs one.

That all depends on the circumstances. I have given cars to many people, but certainly not to everyone who wants one.

Giving someone something might be the wrong thing to do, because each person needs to qualify for his or her own needs.

Giving something to someone who has not qualified for it might destroy him; it might make him a selfish person, because then he would not need to do whatever he is supposed to do to fulfill his mission, and he would not evolve and develop. Somebody else is doing his thinking for him.

Always enter your level, center yourself at alpha, and use that level to make your decisions.

If you feel that you should help someone out, that they are doing what they were sent here to do, and that this will help them, then by all means do it. I help many people, but only when I feel—at my level—that this is the best thing to do.

Remember the old saying about teaching a person how to fish. If you just give a person a fish every day, they may never learn how to fish for themselves.

But if the person is starving, you've got to save their life before they can do anything else. Sometimes people need help. We should certainly help them whenever it is appropriate. That's the reason we are here.

11

Faith: Desire, Belief, and Expectation

Wisdom is the accumulation of feelings of success.

—José Silva

José Silva said that many people talk about the importance of faith. But they don't tell us what faith is, what it is composed of. So he applied his scientific method and his unique insight into examining faith to learn exactly what it is.

He broke faith down into three components:

Desire is the first element of faith. The stronger your desire, the better.

The greater the need—and the more people who will benefit—the greater the desire. The greatest need would be a life-threatening situation.

Belief is next. Do you believe it is possible to accomplish this, and do you believe that you can accomplish it?

Belief comes from successes. The more successes you have, the easier it is to believe you will succeed again.

If you know other people who were in your situation who have done what you want to do, then that increases your belief that it is possible.

The best way to increase your belief that something is possible and you can do it is through your own successes. Every time you program for something and succeed, you increase your belief in your own programming ability.

You can use these successes—and any other successes you have—by entering your level and reviewing them.

Expectation is the third element of faith. Mr. Silva also referred to it as *hope*. That is what you are visualizing in the third scene of the Three-Scenes Technique—what you expect to achieve, what you hope to have.

Expectation is the dream that you have, your goal, the thing that you hope for. Keep a mental picture of it in your mind, and that will help to keep you moving in the right direction, and will help to motivate you to do the work that is necessary.

How to Increase Your Self-Confidence

José Silva said that confidence breeds success. And confidence comes from experience—successful experiences. Here is what he wrote:

> People who are successful, who achieve a great deal, have a certain attitude, a unique feeling of confidence, that is easily identified by other people, particularly other successful people.
>
> Every time you have a success, you get a special feeling that you can obtain only by having success. These feelings of success help build an inner confidence within you that creates a special power to bring you even more success.

When you have that confidence, when you have that unique feeling of success deep within you, you feel differently, you think differently, you act differently than a person who lacks that confidence.

When you have that feeling of confidence and success, you speak out boldly, you offer suggestions without apprehension about the results either to yourself or to others. The words you need come to you, yet your words are only a part of the communication you have with others. Your presence, your bearing, your enthusiasm, your expressions and posture all communicate your confidence, your leadership.

Much of this can be faked, of course; you can learn the language of successful people; you can take acting lessons and learn to play the part of a confident person. This will fool a lot of people, but not people who actually have these qualities.

People who have this inner feeling of confidence, people who know their true value, instinctively recognize others who have it. And they are attracted to each other. The "lucky break" comes to the person who has the inner qualities to take advantage of the opportunity.

How can you develop this inner confidence if you do not have it, and enhance it if you do? How can you become part of this network of successful people who reinforce and help each other?

You can do it by using your inner conscious levels, your alpha brain-wave levels, your alpha level of mind.

Whenever you have a success, even a small success, you will get that unique feeling of success that comes only when you succeed.

Reinforce This Success

Reinforce this success many times. At your alpha level, recall it to mind, relive this success, live it over and over again, recalling the feelings associated with it, and visualizing it over and over.

By doing this at your alpha brain-wave level, and using visualization and imagination, you are developing your right-brain hemisphere. And this is the one big success secret of the most successful people: they use the right brain hemisphere creatively, clairvoyantly, and effectively.

José Silva's Special Advice

We used to say, you reach success with a ladder of failures, to reach your next success.

That's wrong.

We reach greater successes with a ladder of lesser successes. But always your foundation should be success. Not failure.

So enter the alpha level and reinforce your successes to make them appear more frequently and stronger from then on.

Nobody will know the feeling of success until they succeed. There is no way to explain to anybody how it feels to succeed. It is a very unusual feeling, when you succeed.

Wisdom is the accumulation of feelings of success. That's wisdom: the accumulation of feelings of success.

Go to alpha when you have succeeded, go to alpha and strengthen the feeling of success, when you succeeded, the way you succeeded.

Go over whatever you did when you were successful to reinforce it. That's a good foundation to keep on succeeding.

All Successes Are Beneficial

It doesn't matter whether the success benefits you or someone else; it is still a success. It is often easier to help other people solve their problems than for us to solve our own, so a secondary benefit of helping other people is that it will improve your own self-confidence.

As your small successes enable you to accumulate more feelings of success, you will be able to use that energy to have an bigger success. You will begin to have bigger successes, and that will accelerate your progress.

Even if you have only one talent, that is enough. When you use that talent, it will grow, because each time you have a success with that talent, it will add to your feelings of success and bring you that much closer to unlocking a second talent.

When you unlock a second talent and begin accumulating feelings of success with that talent in addition to the first one, your programming ability will grow even faster. That will soon result in you unlocking a third talent, and then a fourth, and more.

When you have a big project to work on, a good approach will be to program steps along the way—benchmarks that let you know you are moving in the right direction. In addition to increasing your ability and your talents, this will also build your confidence and your belief—genuine, deep-seated belief—that you will succeed.

Just saying that you believe something doesn't make it true. It is better than expressing doubt, but real belief comes from successes.

Break Big Projects into Manageable Steps

We recommend breaking big projects down into small steps so that you can get indications of how to proceed.

What would be the first indication that you are moving in the correct direction, something that you could see within the next three days?

Use your level to identify the first thing that needs to happen, something towards which you could see some progress within the next three days.

Then go out and work to make that happen. If you see some progress within that time, then you know you are on the right track; keep going.

If the situation gets worse in the next three days, then go to level and analyze it. Do the opposite of whatever you were doing, and see if that will get things moving in the correct direction.

If nothing happens, then try something different; alter what you are doing. Program more, program less, program at a different time of day, change your images, change what you are trying to accomplish, and see what happens.

Always use your feedback to guide you.

Remember: Visualization is the starting point. Then do the work, and observe what happens, and use the feedback you get to guide your future actions.

A Formula to Boost Your Desire and Enthusiasm

The more you desire something, the harder you will work to get it. All other things being equal, the prize goes to the one who wants it the most. Great coaches and athletes know this, and they know how to motivate themselves and others.

José Silva's brother Juan, the foreign director for Silva International for twenty years, developed a powerful motivational formula as a result of nearly forty years of research, practice, and teaching people how to apply the new science of psychorientology. Here is his advice for increasing your desire for a goal:

> Once you make up your mind that you want something, then you can increase your desire to get it by going to your level and thinking about it.
>
> Besides visualizing the solution image that you have created on your Mental Screen, you can increase your desire by thinking of all the *reasons* you have for reaching your goal.
>
> If you go to level and think of three reasons for reaching your goal, you will have a certain amount of desire. If you keep thinking, and you think of three more reasons for reaching your goal, you will have twice as much desire.
>
> There are many benefits associated with making a sale. You will benefit, of course. So will your customer. So will your family. So will your customer's family. So will the people you purchase things from with the money you earn.

Motivation Technique in Action

Let me give you an example. I recently made a trip to Mexico, and visited the owners of a large factory. I used to manage that factory for them, back in the 1950s. But economic times have been difficult in Mexico, and things have changed.

We visited the factory, and it was very sad for me to see that much of the large manufacturing facility was sitting idle, with fifteen hundred of the employees laid off. The manager of the factory is a very good friend of mine. He is a good manager, but the bad nationwide economic conditions had gotten the best of him.

We left the factory and went to a nearby restaurant to eat lunch. As we talked, my thoughts kept going back to the idle machines in the factory, and to the fifteen hundred employees who were now out of work and not earning money to support themselves and their families the way they desired.

I thought about the merchants in town, such as the owner of the restaurant where we had come to eat, and how their business would be down, since the factory workers had no money coming in. The restaurant should have been crowded during lunchtime, but only a few tables were occupied.

Many people were suffering. How, I wondered, might I help them? Is there anything I can do to help?

I asked my friends to excuse me for a moment and I headed towards the rest room. What I wanted, of course, was time to enter my level and think about possible solutions to the problem. The rest room is an excellent place to do this. It is private. It is quiet. Nobody bothers you. And when you close the door, nobody sees you sitting there with your eyes closed.

When I entered my level, I again thought about all those fifteen hundred employees who were now out of work. I thought about the empty tables at the restaurant, and the restaurant employees who were now also out of work. I thought about other merchants who were also suffering, along with their families, because of the economic problems.

Then, after I had completed my study of the problem, I began to think about possible solutions.

After a few minutes I returned to the table. And I started presenting the ideas that I had thought of at level to the manager of the factory, about where he could find new markets and how he could sell to them.

The ideas made sense to him. He began to get excited. In fact, he even got me involved by getting me to agree to use some of my contacts in other countries to help him get started.

"After you came back from the rest room," the manager told me, "you did not want to listen to me anymore. You just wanted to tell me your ideas."

I agreed. "That's right. I'd heard all I needed to hear about the problems. I wanted to offer some solutions."

"I don't know what you found in that rest room," my friend said. "It must have been some kind of think tank, because you sure came back with a lot of good ideas. Thank you for caring."

That's the key to the technique I use: I care.

In order for me to get a strong motivation so that creative ideas for solutions to problems will come, I need to think about all the people who will benefit. In this case, it was not just my friend's son who now manages the factory; it was also the fifteen hundred employees, their families, and more.

I had seen things that made me want to help. I had heard the stories of hardship, and I wanted to help. I had imagined what it must be like, and how I would feel if I were in that position and was worried about my employees and how they must be worried about supporting their families, and I wanted to help. I thought about the children of the laid-off employees and how they must have felt, not having new shoes to wear to school, not having money for necessary things, much less extras.

I had a very strong desire to help, because so many people would benefit. When you have that kind of desire to help, and you take action, then you will help solve any problem that exists.

It is much easier to program for a necessity than for a luxury. And when the need is as urgent, as it was in my friend's factory, then you are almost always guaranteed of success in your programming.

It will still take a lot of work to build up enough new business to put everyone back to work. It will still take a lot more programming to make the correct decisions, to intuitively sense the needs and how best to fill them. But it can be done.

Also remember that learning to program successfully is just like learning any other skill: You have to actually do it; you have to practice it to learn how to do it; and the more you do it, the better you get.

Part Four

How to Influence Others

12

Your Power to Influence

*We will not program those who block us, or soon you get where
you want to control other people. We don't want to control anybody.*

—José Silva

Everybody knows about the so-called five physical senses. We now
know that there are more than five. Have you ever stared at somebody, at the back of their head perhaps, and eventually they turn
and look at you? Or perhaps you are the one who was stared at,
and you detected it.

That happens with the physical part of your aura. Your body
radiates energy, both physical and nonphysical, and other people
can detect it.

When you know what to do, you can use the physical part of
your aura to influence people who are in the vicinity.

They might also be influencing you, whether they know it or
not. Have you ever started to feel nervous and not known why? It
could be that you are detecting someone else's mood through their
aura transmission.

It is easy to control what you transmit and what you receive through the aura, once you understand how it works and know what to do.

This ability can be a valuable tool in helping you to make a good first impression, improve your relationships, and even detect what other people are thinking and feeling.

It is not just humans who are affected by your aura radiation. Everything in the vicinity is impressed with information that is transmitted automatically by your aura. There are many ways you can use this beneficially.

Let's turn the floor over to José Silva to tell us what he learned about the human aura while conducting his trailblazing research into the mind and human potential.

You Can Learn to Use Your Aura to Help You

Here's a short quiz:

Why is your body like a radio?

Because both are communications devices.

Your body radiates energy, called an *aura*, just as a radio station radiates electromagnetic waves that carry a radio program.

I spent much of my life repairing radios and other electronic equipment. When I began to learn about the human mind and the body's aura, my experience with electronics came in very handy.

It helped me to understand some of the ways that we communicate, ways that most people don't yet fully understand.

Your body is a much more sophisticated communications station than a radio transmitter. You can communicate with:

- Words
- The tone and inflection of your voice
- Your eyes
- Your body language
- Your hands
- Your aura
- Your mind

The first six kinds of communication that we've listed here are limited by time and space. People have to be able to hear you or see you, or be within range of your aura.

The seventh kind of communication—your mind and your psychic ability—has no limits, as far as we know. You can communicate with anyone, anywhere, instantly, with your mind.

There are plenty of books and courses to help you with the first five types of communication.

Now I want to talk about the other two.

Your Aura

The human body radiates seven energy fields. The combined energy fields are called the human aura.

The human aura is modulated by brain activity.

To modulate means to change, to alter in some way.

A radio transmitter transmits a carrier signal.

The information to be transmitted—the announcer's voice, for instance, or the music being played—is combined with the carrier signal and alters the carrier signal.

The radio that receives this combined signal then strips away the carrier signal and is left with only the information that was added to it.

Your aura is modulated by your brain activity. Your brain is modulated by thoughts. Every thought that you have alters—modulates—your aura.

Your Aura Penetrates and Alters Matter

The objective part of your aura radiates out about eight meters—about twenty-five feet—from your body. Anyone within that range can detect your aura.

That's why, when a person who is very upset comes into a room, you can "feel" their presence even before you see them or hear them.

You can influence people around you by your own thoughts. If you are happy and at peace, your aura will reflect this, and will tend to influence other people's auras to be happy and peaceful.

The aura energy penetrates both inanimate and animate matter, causing an alteration in matter.

Inanimate matter retains the alteration.

Animate matter continues to evolve in an altered state.

Several Ways to Detect Information

We can detect this energy field in two forms:

1. What can be seen
2. What can be felt

And always, always, what can be felt is the stronger of the two.

For instance, we can see a lighted candle from an airplane, in the desert, at great distances, but we cannot see the heat. We can only see the flame.

To feel the heat, we need to get so close.

It is the same thing with the human aura: we can detect it with testing equipment at great distances, but you are not involved with the aura. You are detecting it.

When you get near enough to feel it, then you are involved with the aura.

You can be affected by the aura.

You cannot be affected by seeing it, but you can be affected by feeling it.

When the aura vibrates, this radiation of the aura alters matter, whether inanimate, or plant cell life, or animal cell life, or human cell life. It makes changes.

It alters it.

When we alter inanimate matter, it stays in its altered state, because it doesn't change on its own. It changes because we change it.

But animate life, once it is altered, continues to grow in the altered state. It evolves in the altered state, not in the way it was originally meant to evolve. It is going to somehow alter the growth of the plant, or the animal, or whatever it is we are dealing with, if they are within the aura range of the human being who's at 10 cycles.

When we alter—or program—inanimate matter, it stays altered. If we alter it again, it stays altered.

But if we alter a plant that's growing, it grows. We alter it again, it grows. We alter it again, it continues to grow, in the altered direction.

So we can with mind create a model to imagine that the plant will be altered in this direction, so we can imagine—to the left—that plant moving in that direction, and before you know it, it is going to grow in that direction, because we caused the altering effect, through the aura radiation, if the aura is reaching the plant.

We can help, and we can function within natural laws— having natural laws to back us up—if we are not destroying the plant, if we are helping it to get where it should grow faster, to produce a bloom faster, to produce more fruit faster. We can help it do that.

But at a distance, beyond the range of the aura—the physical part of the aura—beyond that we can only help it to grow faster, to do better what it can do.

Within the aura range we can destroy the plant too, because of the physical body radiation.

Physical body radiation can help or it can hurt.

The spiritual body radiation can only help; it cannot hurt.

The spiritual part has no limitations in distance.

The physical part is limited by distance, just as radio waves are limited depending on how strong the station is.

A station of 50,000 watts can be heard over here but not over there. Energy dissipates with distance.

Same thing with the aura, the physical part of the aura.

But the spiritual part of the aura has no limitations in distance.

That's what helps the plant to grow faster, not to destroy it.

It is the physical part that can destroy. But it only destroys within a limited range, not beyond that range.

So that's the negative part of the physical aura. It can function in a negative way.

The spiritual, subjective part of the aura always works only in a constructive way.

Thought Modulation

There are several different frequencies that the brain operate on:

- Beta, the outer conscious level, which is ideal for taking action in the physical world.
- Alpha, the inner conscious level (formerly the subconscious), the strongest, most rhythmic frequency, ideal for thinking.
- Theta, a lower frequency.
- Delta, associated with deep sleep and communication with higher intelligence in a pure spiritual dimension, on the "other side," as we say.

Thinking modulates the brain at various frequencies: the beta brain-wave frequencies, and also at the lower alpha brain-wave frequencies.

The energy transmitted when thought modulates the brain at the beta frequency is limited by distance. This energy, a physical energy, can be used either to help or to harm. It can attract animate matter back to a normal condition, or force matter into an abnormal condition.

This is what happens when a psychic bends a spoon: the normal is changed to the abnormal, through the use of the physical part of the body's aura radiation. That's why we don't teach or practice spoon bending; we prefer to change the abnormal to the normal.

When thoughts modulate the brain at the alpha frequency, then distance is no barrier. When doing this, you can help, but you cannot harm. You can change the abnormal back to the normal, but you cannot change the normal to the abnormal with this subjective (nonphysical) energy.

It takes physical energy to cause physical harm, to change the normal to the abnormal. Physical energy works by repulsion.

Subjective energy cannot exert force against physics. Subjective energy can only work through attraction. It attracts animate matter to return to a normal condition, to conform to the original spiritual blueprint for that particular object.

The modulation is stronger when thought is accompanied by imagination.

The most effective programming is done when thought, accompanied by imagination, modulates the brain at the alpha level, where there is the most energy, and where distance is no barrier.

Examining the Aura

The human aura is made up of seven fields of energy:

The first is spiritual, 99 percent of which is controlled by the "other side," from the spiritual dimension.

The next three—subatomic, atomic, and part of the molecular—are controlled from the right brain hemisphere. However, the molecular evolves into the physical, and is partially controlled by the left brain hemisphere.

The final three—cells, organs, and organ systems—are controlled from the left brain hemisphere.

In order to live a normal life, the way God intended, we must learn to control the energy fields correctly, that is, we must use the right brain hemisphere appropriately.

Solving Problems

Most people, approximately 90 percent, cannot use the alpha

part of the brain deductively, to analyze information and solve problems.

In the Silva UltraMind ESP System, everyone learns, with just a few hours of training, how to think deductively at the alpha level, and then take action at the beta brain-wave level. That is what you are learning to do in this book.

Once you have access to both regions of your brain, and you have learned how to activate your mind while remaining at the alpha level, then you have tremendous programming capability.

Your thoughts will modulate your aura, so that everyone around you is influenced in a positive direction. This will make your life much easier.

And you are also able to project your thoughts great distances, through the use of the right brain hemisphere, so that you can influence people and events that are not in your physical presence. [You can master that skill using the book *Silva UltraMind Systems ESP for Business Success*.]

By Chance or by Choice?

Your aura is automatically influencing people around you, whether you know it or not.

The question is: what kind of influence is it?

What kind of people do you attract into your life? This can give you an idea of what kind of message you are putting out through your aura.

When you learn to function at the alpha level with the System we have designed, you become more sensitive both at detecting information that can affect your life, and at programming to correct problems.

Unfortunately, 90 percent of the people on the planet live their lives more by chance than by choice. They hope that good things will happen to them, but all too often they don't.

People who use both brain hemispheres have the ability to take greater control over their own lives, and to be healthier, happier, and more successful.

If you are not one of the fortunate 10 percent who are "naturals," you need not despair. Simply practice the techniques you are learning in this book and you will be able to do all that the naturals can do . . . and probably even more.

It is how God intended us to live—using all of the equipment that we were given, using both brain hemispheres, using both the beta and the alpha levels consciously, to detect information and to correct problems.

Aura Communication in Action

You've seen them—people who seem able to impose their will on others, who "sense" what to say and what to do. Great entertainers are naturals at this. There was an excellent example of this in an interview with violinist Joshua Bell on Tavis Smiley's PBS television program on October 12, 2016.

Smiley started by observing that in classical music concerts, "it's not until the very end that you discover whether or not the audience was with you by how long the ovation is, how boisterous it is, how many curtain calls you make." Then he asked the violinist, "How do you know, what's that feeling you get, to know whether or not the audience is 'getting' you, whether they're with you?"

"It's a really good question," Bell replied, "because it's really hard to understand it myself, but I can feel it."

"You can feel it, though?" Smiley said.

"Absolutely can feel it."

"When you're on and when you're off?" Smiley continued.

"Both," Bell said. "I can certainly feel when I'm off. But I can feel the audience hanging on every note. That's the thing about classical music. Again, you need that participation from the audience. . . . I can still feel it, you know, whether they're listening to and feeling that something is being comprehended on their end. And it's very hard to describe how one feels.

"It's a kind of energy, this magical energy that, when they're really expectant and feeling like waiting for the next note to come, it just makes me want to play better, and I feel like I'm inside it."

Bell also spoke about how much that kind of communication from the audience means to him. "It makes a big difference to have an audience that kind of understands, or at least is there participating. I mean, it's all about that back and forth.

"So that kind of exchange is what I live for. That's why I love live performance, I have to say, more than recordings. You try to recreate that in a recording session. You play for your colleagues that are playing with you, but there's nothing like that live feel."

How You Can Influence Others with Your Aura

If you have been practicing the Silva Centering Exercise as instructed in chapter 1, then you have now learned how to do your thinking and to function dynamically at the alpha level, with conscious awareness.

You are also learning how to control the alpha level, and how to use it whenever you desire to help you solve problems and make the world a better place to live. This is something that many of the natural alpha thinkers don't know how to do. With them, it is more hit or miss.

Now that you have this ability, what do you need to do in order to interact with an audience, and to influence them for the common good?

It is very simple:

First, you enter the alpha level, as you have learned.

Second, you pre-program yourself by visualizing what you need to accomplish. The Three-Scenes Technique that you learned in chapter 4 is an excellent way to do this. So is Mental Rehearsal, described in chapter 5.

Third, you put your ideas into action and do what you programmed. When you are interacting with others, visualize the image of what you want—the image you created in the third scene of the Three-Scenes Technique. Project this image with full confidence that this is the outcome you will achieve.

That is what Tracy Kay Huddleston did when she wanted to meet two of her heroes. (We've already seen how Tracy Kay used Silva methods to heal her scoliosis.) Here is her story:

Young Woman Impresses Her Heroes

"For programming confidence," Tracy Kay said, "I envisioned myself in situations I'd often be nervous in, such as making a speech or making new friends, and pictured myself having confidence and doing great in the situations."

This paid off for her in a very big way when she had an opportunity to meet two authors that she had long admired. She said:

I was last in line at the book signing with the authors, which gave me at least roughly half an hour to prep for talking with them. I built the confidence to talk to them by visualizing being able to strike up a solid conversation with them, which ended up working quite well, because by the time it was my turn we went from simple hellos to a full-blown conversation that went on for at least fifteen or twenty minutes.

They were very interested in me, and by the end both of them were giving me hugs. They didn't talk this long with anyone else, and I don't believe they gave out hugs to any others either, so I'd say it went great! They were both easy to talk to.

Something as important to me as a conversation with my favorite author would have been a situation in which I likely would have relied on my mother for support in the past due to nerves, but my mom was standing on the other side of the room the entire time, and I easily and effortlessly held a conversation without getting nervous. It showed that I had made a big step in better confidence.

As for tips for better communication, what worked for me was playing it all out in my mind first with very positive results: I speak perfectly and they respond perfectly, like a well-written movie!

In reality you have to start somewhere, so on this occasion I began with a big smile and a confident "Hello." When they responded kindly, I knew I could do this and felt more at ease.

I asked questions to determine their interests and found that we had a lot in common, and that kept the conversation going. Sometimes getting others to talk first and then asking questions to keep them talking gives you the time to respond in a favorable manner. Having a good conversation doesn't mean you have to do all of the talking.

Become a More Charismatic Speaker

If you would like to be a more persuasive and charismatic speaker, here is a technique that many Silva instructors use when presenting their seminars.

José Silva named it the Three-Fingers Technique. It can be used for many purposes. In the original Silva Mind Control course, it was used to help students make stronger impressions of their school lessons on their brain neurons, and then to help them recall the information.

Silva instructors sometimes use it that way, but more often they use it to help them have better rapport with their students.

Here is how to use it:

Enter your level as you have learned. Once at your level, bring together the tips of the first two fingers of either hand—or both hands if you wish—with the thumb of that hand. Be sure you use the tips of your fingers and thumb, and not the flat part where your fingerprints are. It is like you are making a circle with your fingers and thumb. You don't have to use any pressure. Just touch your fingertips together.

Then program yourself that "whenever I bring together the tips of my first two fingers and thumb of either hand, as I am doing now, my mind will adjust to a deeper level of awareness for stronger programming."

Then program that whenever you use the Three-Fingers Technique in this manner, this will immediately and automatically reinforce the solution that you have created in the third scene of the Three-Scenes Technique.

Later, when you plan to meet with someone, or to speak to a group, you can use the Three-Scenes Technique to program for a successful outcome with everyone benefiting and the best thing being done for everyone concerned. Keep your three fingers together while doing your programming.

Later, when you are speaking and interacting with the person or persons, all you need to do is to bring together the tips of the thumb and first two fingers of either hand and visualize (recall) the solution image you created in the third scene, and project your mental image to your audience with full confidence that this, or something better, will be the outcome.

Many people refer to this as a "trigger mechanism," because when you do it, it triggers a specific response.

José Silva explained it this way at an training session for new Silva instructors:

The Three-Fingers Technique is a trigger mechanism that reminds you of something that you have programmed before.

If you want to give a lecture to an audience, and you are uptight about it, or concerned, program it, reinforce it, before you enter the stage, with the Three-Fingers Technique. Then while there, hold the Three-Fingers Technique with one hand, or the other hand, and rattle off your lecture. It will come to you easier. You will be more calm, have a more natural delivery.

Always believe that you have something of value to pass on to others. It doesn't matter how you present it, just as long as you transfer the information and the understanding that's of value, that they can use for themselves, and benefit by it. They don't care how you give it to them, just as long as they understand it, and are able to use it from there on.

Additional Applications for the Trigger Mechanism

This technique, like all the others, has applications far beyond the examples given here. Here are some others:

- When you are going to a meeting, use your Three-Fingers Technique to help you remember what you need to remember, and to respond in the most appropriate and beneficial manner.

- Use it when negotiating, to help achieve a positive outcome for everyone involved. Remember to comply with the Laws of Programming that we covered in chapter 10. As José Silva said, "We don't want to gain at someone else's loss; we want to gain while helping the other person to also gain."

- If you get into a disagreement, or an argument, with a family member for instance, use your Three-Fingers Technique to help you remain calm, to understand what the real problem is, and to take the most appropriate action so that everyone will be satisfied.

It is best if you pre-program for the specific situation. For instance, if you get into arguments from time to time, then go to your level and analyze the problem. You will get more ideas at your level than you will at beta. Perhaps you will understand the real reason that is causing the arguments. That alone may be enough to solve the problem.

However, if you are concerned that you may get involved in another argument, then pre-program yourself with the Three-Fingers Technique so that you will respond the way that you desire.

Many Silva instructors, especially when first starting out, program themselves that they will say the right thing at the right time when presenting the course. We program to serve the needs of the people in the class. We also program to answer questions in a way that helps the people who ask them.

An Adaptation for Combat

José Silva modified the Three-Fingers Technique for his son Tony when he was drafted and ordered to go to Vietnam during the Vietnam War.

Mr. Silva explained that it would be difficult to keep the tips of your three fingers together when you are fighting, or firing a rifle. So he programmed a different way.

What he did was to have Tony press the little finger of his hand into the palm of his hand. This is what happens naturally when you make a fist. It is also an easy position when you are firing a rifle: your forefinger is on the trigger, and you can hold the tip of your little finger against the palm of your hand.

He pre-programmed that whenever Tony held the little finger of either hand against the palm of that hand, he would be more intuitive, and aware of any dangerous situation.

How did the technique work? It worked great! Tony told us a story about coming to a fork in the road and selecting one path over another, and learning later that there were Vietcong soldiers waiting to ambush them on the path they avoided.

Mr. Silva programmed about thirty young men from Laredo along with his own son. The area that they were sent to had such a bad reputation that when new soldiers arrived that the paperwork was prepared for their Purple Hearts, with only the date left blank. But all of the young men from Laredo, using their "Little Finger in the Palm of the Hand Technique," came home safely.

Family, Parents, and Children

A human being is not one who looks like one,
it is one who acts like one.

—José Silva

For many people, the most important relationship in their lives is their family relationship.

Although the things you say and do affect your family relationships, your thoughts and feelings also have an effect. Your thoughts and feelings are transmitted through your aura radiation, as we described in chapter 12. José Silva explained it this way:

A big portion of the attraction between male and female comes through the aura.

Have you ever met a person of the opposite sex and immediately felt attracted to them, even though at first glance they would not seem to be your type? This happens to most people. It is the influence of the aura.

When you meet the right person, you know it immediately, because of the way you feel. This is the influence of the two auras coming together in a certain way.

Once the boy and girl start dating each other, their auras begin a process of trying to alter the other person's aura. Eventually, both are altered a certain amount, until they are equal and in harmony with each other.

That's why it is important for couples to stay physically close to each other. They should sleep in the same bed.

If one person starts seeing another person, then their aura changes, and it is no longer in complete harmony with their original partner's aura. Then the original partners grow apart.

Use the Silva Techniques to Improve Your Relationships

You can influence your family members and your relationship with them in a positive way by doing the things we have been talking about:

Use the powerful alpha level as you learned in chapter 1 to analyze your interactions with family members to help you understand why they—and you—do the things you do.

Always use positive language and positive thoughts when interacting with family members, the way you learned in chapter 2. It is easy to complain and say, "Why are you always so impatient?" What mental picture does that create?

Better to say, "I always appreciate it when you are patient with me." Remember to create the mental images of what you want, and project those mental images to the other person, as you learned in chapter 3.

You can go to your level at any time and use the Three-Scenes Technique that you learned in chapter 4 to correct problems in your relationships. You can also teach your loved ones how to go to level, and then you can go to level together and work on your relationship.

Sometimes our insecurities interfere with our ability to accept good things that come into our lives, like loving relationships. At your level you can often recognize when this is happening, and make corrections the way we discussed in chapters 5, 6, and 8.

If you are doing something that annoys your loved ones—or if you forget to do things that they like—you can use the techniques in chapter 7 to change your habits.

You can easily understand how all of the things we discussed in part 3 of this book can help you build strong, loving relationships. When you need help to do that, you can call on higher intelligence for guidance.

Keep in mind what you learned in chapter 12 about how you can affect people both positively and negatively with the physical part of your aura when they are nearby.

You can even affect them when they are not nearby by programming things in the environment either negatively or positively with the physical part of your aura.

One of our associates, Dr. Bernard Grad, conducted some very significant research that shows just how important it is to maintain a positive attitude at all time.

Babies Need Mothers

In chapter 6 Dr. Clancy McKenzie explained how he helped combat veterans deal with PTSD. His work with those veterans, combined with insights he gained while at the alpha level, led to his discovery of the cause of schizophrenia and depression.

He realized that very early childhood experiences could set the stage for the later development of psychoses and nonpsychotic depressions. He explained:

> For as long as mammals have populated the earth, separation from mother has meant death.
>
> Therefore separation from the mother can be more terrifying to a baby than war trauma is to a soldier.
>
> Instead of a loud noise precipitating the flashback to a war trauma, it is a separation from some other "most important person," usually during adolescence, that precipitates the initial flashback.
>
> This represents a partial return to the earlier mind, brain, reality, feelings, behavior, chemistry, physiology, body movements, level of affective expression, and to the anatomic sites in the brain that were active and developing at the precise time of the original traumas. Thus the earlier developmental brain structures become reactivated, while the later developmental ones undergo disuse atrophy.
>
> While the person might not remember the fear of Mother leaving him or her, emotions are far more intense than thoughts, and the intense self-hatred rises to the surface without the actual memory of thinking, "Mommy left me because I could not please her."
>
> For example, a family brought a young man to me who was convinced he never would be able to walk again because his feet hurt. That was more real to him than the reality that he had just walked into my office. I told the family something happened to

him when he was just twelve months old. "Nothing happened," they replied. I insisted it did, and they insisted it didn't. Finally, I exclaimed: "Something happened to cause his mother to be extremely upset when he was just twelve months old!" One replied, "Oh, his older brother died then." Obviously, with the death of her older son, the mother would have been devastated and emotionally separated from the baby for a period of time.

The mechanism is the same for all the disorders, from schizophrenia to non-psychotic depression. Only the age of origin differs, and the symptoms match the age of origin.

The age of origin of that one is easy to surmise. In the United States, children are learning to walk when they are twelve months old. Walking is new to them, so their feet hurt. He said his feet hurt, and he believed that he couldn't walk, even though he had walked into my office.

Here are some suggestions from Dr. McKenzie about what a mother can do to minimize the risk of inadvertently causing her child to feel abandoned if she has to turn her attention to something else.

The first thing is to remember if you are planning to have a child, that you and your love and attention are the most important things in the child's life, especially for the first twenty-four to thirty-six months. Be sure to go to your center, the alpha level, and communicate your love and commitment to your baby.

If you have an emergency that requires your attention, enter the alpha level and reassure you baby that she or he is still the most important thing in your life and you are still there with your love and protection. Use mental pictures to communicate this to your child.

If you feel that you have to go to work to earn enough money to take care of the child, or if you want to try to fulfill your parenting responsibilities while also having a career, here are some things you can do.

When you are away from your baby, enter the alpha level frequently and use mental pictures to communicate your love and commitment to your child.

Perhaps you and your baby's father can work different shifts so that one of you is always there with the baby.

Perhaps there is another relative, like a grandmother, who is reliable and consistent and who can watch over the child the same as you would if you were there. A busy day-care center that doesn't have enough people to provide constant attention for each child is not a good choice.

If a baby sitter is necessary, this must be handled very carefully. The mother needs to spend some time observing the baby sitter to make sure the baby is comfortable with the baby sitter, and that the baby sitter enjoys being with the baby. Start slowly, leaving your baby with the sitter for a short period of time, and gradually increase the time to insure that your baby knows that you are going to come back.

If your employer provides day-care services on site, be sure check in as often as possible so your child can see you, and to be sure that someone at the daycare center is paying attention to your child.

On the days that are not at your job, spend time with your child. If you begin to feel overwhelmed, then use the Silva Centering Exercise to enter your level, relax, and program to fulfill your responsibilities enthusiastically and effectively. Remember the benefits of having a child and the joy you will experience later when your child has grown into a productive and successful member of society. Doing this is very rejuvenating.

Following our guidance will help ensure that your child will grow up healthy and well adjusted.

For more information on this subject, read Dr. McKenzie's book *Babies Need Mothers: How Mothers Can Prevent Mental Illness In Their Children* and visit his website: www.AlternativeAPA.com.

How Your Thoughts and Emotions Affect Everything in Your Environment

The following is taken from a transcript of the proceedings of a two-day conference called "The Mind in Search of Itself," sponsored by Mind Science Foundation and Silva International in Washington, D.C., November 25–26, 1972. Bernard Grad, PhD was an associate professor of gerontology at McGill University School of Medicine, Montreal, Canada. He has published seventy papers in the fields of aging, cancer, and endocrinology.

This all started when a Hungarian gentleman (Mr. E.) came to me with the claim to be able to accelerate healing in people according to his experience in Hungary. I told him I was a biologist and therefore I couldn't bring any patients to him, but we could do experiments on animals and on plants.

When I asked him how he worked, he said that all he did was to lay his hands on the people. If they had a headache, he would put his hands on the head. He would hold his hands there for a while, fifteen minutes, or twenty minutes, and repeat this as required, perhaps the next day or several times a week, generally not on the same day.

When we began to think of how we would do these experiments on animals, I preferred to work with mice. They're small and therefore inexpensive to maintain.

Such studies were conducted both in our lab and in the Department of Physiology of the University of Manitoba. The results of this experiment were published in the *International Journal of Parapsychology* and in the *Journal for the American Society of Psychical Research*.

RESEARCH WITH PLANTS

In plants, we began our studies just as we did with mice. That is, we wanted to see if we could affect healthy plants.

The first plant experiment showed that the laying on of hands–treated group had more seedlings coming through the soil initially than did the controls, and that they grew faster and yielded more plant material than the controls. And all this was supported by statistical analysis.

The details of the technique are written up in publications in the two journals mentioned previously. However, the main point which should be mentioned here is that it was not necessary to have Mr. E. or Mr. B. [another subject] hold the plant pots in the hands to treat them.

It was possible to treat them just by holding between the hands the 1 percent saline solution to be poured over them. [. . .]

EFFECT OF MENTAL ATTITUDE

We now come to the last experiment, which was also done on plants. It was designed to test whether saline solutions held by a person who was positive in his feeling, and genuinely and naturally so, not psyched up to be so, would have a positive effect on plants watered with it; whereas a person who was depressed would have the opposite effect.

Now to test this, we did the following experiment:

There were four groups, 18 pots per group, with 20 barley seeds in each pot. That means there were 360 seeds per group and there were four such groups, that is, 1,440 seeds in the entire experiment.

Now one of the groups was a control group which received only untreated 1 percent saline solution, the bottle not being held for 30 minutes by anyone. This 1 percent saline, by the way, was the kind that is used by hospitals to give infusions to patients. It was sterile, non-pyrogenic and under vacuum.

In addition to the control bottle, three more were used in the experiment, each held by a different person.

THE RESEARCH SUBJECTS

One of these people was Mr. B. He has a passion for plants and is able to make them grow and thrive.

The other two people were depressive patients in the hospital where I worked. One of them had a psychotic depression and the other one had a neurotic depression.

I had obtained permission from their doctors to give them each a bottle to hold, during which time the bottle was to be in a brown paper bag as part of the multiblind system of the experiment. Each person was asked to hold the bottle for half an hour.

I gave the bottle to Mr. B. with the necessary explanation and I was ready to provide the same to the two patients.

When I came to the man who was the more deeply depressed of the two, he didn't even ask me why I was giving him the bottle. I was wearing a white coat, as I usually do, and he thought I was a medical doctor coming to prepare him for electric shock therapy and he told me he didn't need any.

I tried to explain to him that I wasn't there to prepare him for this but that all I wanted him to do was to hold the bottle in his hands for half an hour, but he appeared not to believe me and didn't bother to ask what was in the bottle; therefore, I didn't bother to explain. I just asked somebody to keep an eye on him during the time he held the bottle and I said I would be back in half an hour.

This man, I want to emphasize, was definitely depressed at this point in time and certainly in a negative state of mind.

The other patient was a young woman. When I came to see her she had a neurotic depression. She was depressed, but less severely so than the man, and she was sitting somewhat forlornly in an out-patient department.

When I came up to her and asked her if she would be kind enough to hold the bottle for half an hour, she was a little taken aback and asked, "Well, why are you giving me this to hold?"

I told her that this was part of an experiment; we wanted her to hold the bottle in her hand and later on we wanted to put the saline solution on some plants.

She thought this was a great idea and she brightened right up and this upset me, because I didn't want her to become enthusiastic. In fact, I chose her for the experiment just for the opposite reasons. So there we were and the die was cast and I decided we would just go ahead with the experiment.

When I came back half an hour later she was faithfully holding the bottle, somewhat like a mother holding a child, I thought, in a kind of cradling fashion. I didn't know what to make of all of this but I was going to see what would happen in any case.

The man with the psychotic depression was still busy engaging me in conversation about his not needing electric shock therapy and I departed without further explanation.

THE WATERING EXPERIMENT

We then proceeded to do the experiments.

The multiblind system was so extensive that one of my worries was whether I could get all of the pieces of information together again without having mixed the information up. When the information was decoded, it was a source of relief that there was no mix-up at all.

What was even more astonishing to me (and I have had experience in this field) was that the results did turn out mostly as I had hypothesized.

Thus, the group that grew the slowest was the one watered by saline held by the man with the psychotic depression; the next lowest group was the untreated control, the bottle not held by anybody; and the next lowest group was that of the girl who had the neurotic depression. The best one was Mr. B.'s group.

Now, I had supposed that this girl's plants would grow more slowly than the control, but this was not so, and I attribute this to the fact that she was quite enthusiastic about the experiment.

The interesting thing is it is not the diagnosis which is important for this experiment; what is important is the state of mind you are in at the moment.

EMOTIONS CAN BE STORED IN MATTER

There are quite a few implications arising from this study.

Perhaps the most critical implication of all is the fact that it says that anybody handling any material imparts to that material something that bears a relation to his emotional state.

I assume that some energy was at the core of this transfer, for it took place through the glass wall of the bottle containing the saline solution.

Our earlier experiments on goiter and wound healing also suggested that such energy transfers can occur between man and animal, and I'm sure also between man and man. If this is accepted, it would help to explain why some physicians are more effective than others (this has something to do with what we call the bedside manner) and why some nurses, for example, can have a profound effect on patients, depending on what their attitude is.

Also, we know for example in psychotherapy, where a patient comes to a doctor repeatedly, that there is a kind of relationship that develops between psychiatrist and patient which Freud called transference. Now, I believe there is an energy process at work here; and I think that this process is at work between parents and children, teachers and students, man and wife, and in the old days between the pharmacist and the medication he prepared.

Some children are very disturbed because there is a lack of . . . we call it rapport.

Rapport describes an energy process, I believe—something passing between parent and child which may be positive or the opposite.

Then there is the relationship of a mother to cooking. She has a responsibility there, and I can expand further on this, but time does not allow.

Research into Primary Perception at the Cell Level

Another researcher who demonstrated that plants react to our emotions was Cleve Backster. Backster was a polygraph (lie detector) expert and became a big supporter of José Silva's work. His research into "primary perception" started late one night when he decided to connect his polygraph to a plant and see if he could get the plant to react.

First he watered the plant with the idea of testing to see if the polygraph could detect how long it took the water to travel up the long stem of the plant and reach the leaves. The polygraph did not respond the way Backster had expected.

"The tracings on the printout had the contour of a human being tested," he said, "reacting the way a person does when you are asking a question that could get them in trouble.

"So I forgot about the rising water time and said to myself, 'Wow, this thing wants to show me people-like reactions. So I began to wonder what I could do that would be a threat to the well-being of the plant, similar to the fact that a relevant question regarding a crime could be a threat to a person taking a polygraph test if they're lying."

Then the idea occurred to him that he could burn the plant. "I didn't have matches in the room," he said. "I wasn't touching the plant in any way. I was maybe five feet away from the desk. The only new thing that occurred was my intent to burn that plant leaf.

"In an instant, when I *thought* of burning that plant leaf and the image entered my mind, the polygraph went into a wild agitation.

"Now this was very late at night and towards morning. The building was empty and there was just no other reason for this reaction. I thought, 'Wow! This thing read my mind!' It was that obvious to me right then, and my consciousness hasn't been the same since."

Backster learned another very valuable lesson when other scientists started trying to replicate his experiment. One scientist called and told him it didn't work. The scientist had used the same kind of plant, the same equipment, had done everything exactly the way Backster had. Or at least he thought he did.

"Did you intend to burn the plant?" Backster asked. The scientists said no, that Backster didn't burn the plant, so there was no need to.

"But I *intended* to burn the plant," Backster told him. "There is a difference between 'pretend' and 'intend.'"

That is important to remember when you want to influence someone. If you are trying out our techniques just to see how they work, you might not get satisfying results.

But when you have a critical need to influence somebody—a life-or-death situation, for instance—then even if you don't have much skill with the technique, you can still get excellent results, the way that Joe Girard finally managed to persuade somebody to buy a car when he was desperate to buy groceries for his wife and baby. (His story is in chapter 8.)

Remember what Juan Silva told us in chapter 11 about boosting your desire and enthusiasm. When your intention is to help people without demanding benefits for yourself in return, your intention will communicate and you will get results.

For more information about Cleve Backster's work into primary perception at the cell level, visit www.CleveBackster.com.

What a French Pharmacist Taught Us about the Mind

In the early years of the twentieth century a French chemist—today we would call him a pharmacist—named Émile Coué gained an understanding that the human mind can play as powerful a role in healing the body as the drugs he was preparing and dispensing to people.

He developed a hypnosislike system that he called *autosuggestion* so that he could guide people to the correct level of mind and brain activity and then mentally communicate a "program" that would stimulate the patient's brain to correct the abnormalities in their body. Then he sent them home with instructions to repeat a statement every morning: "Every day in every respect I am getting better and better."

That was not just some platitude; it was not some sort of affirmation made consciously that was then supposed to influence the subconscious in some mysterious way, as some people mistakenly think. How could it? How could something you do consciously influence the subconscious?

Coué used the statement as a reinforcing mechanism to activate the program that he had "installed" in the patient's brain.

José Silva studied what Coué had done, and when his own research produced a System to teach people how to unleash the potential of their own mind, he paid tribute to Coué and his breakthrough contributions to the field by adopting Coué's slogan as the slogan for his own System:

Every day, in every way, I am getting better, better, and better.

Silva added one more "better" to indicate that we continue to gain more and more understanding. "Scientific discoveries are always semiconclusions," he said. "When you get a bigger tele-scope, you discover more planets."

In addition to using his slogan, Silva carried Coué's concept one step further in applying the "better and better" statement as a reinforcing mechanism. Silva students mentally repeat the better and better statement every time they enter the alpha level in order to associate it with the benefits and power of that level of mind, so that when they repeat it later at the outer, beta brain-wave level, it reinforces all of the programming that they have done at the alpha level.

So when you ask a Silva graduate how they are doing and they answer, "Better and better, thank you, how are you?" they are not "affirming," they are not "hoping" to get better; they are *activating the programming* that they have done consciously at the alpha level. When you do that, every benefit of your functioning at the alpha level will be reinforced every time you repeat that statement.

Education and Correction of Children

Every parent knows what a great blessing—and a great respon-sibility—it is to have children. Both Émile Coué and José Silva developed techniques to help you guide and protect your children. Here are some of them.

Both men said that the education of a child should begin before birth.

"When do you think that the education of your genius child should begin?" José Silva asks. "It should begin as soon as you know there is a pregnancy. Enter your level and talk to your unborn child."

Coué said that "if a prospective mother, a few weeks after conception, will make a mental picture of the child she expects to bring into the world, concerning the physical and moral qualities with which she desires her offspring to be endowed, and if she will then continue to hold that mental image during the time of gestation, the child will have the qualities desired.

"A child thus conceived will more readily accept good suggestions and transform them into autosuggestions which may determine the course of its life," Coué continued. "For you must realize that all our words and all our acts are but the results of autosuggestions induced, for the most part, through suggestion by means of example or speech."

What and How to Teach

"In dealing with children," Coué explained, "always be even-tempered and speak to them in gentle but firm tones. In this way you influence them to be obedient without arousing the slightest desire to resist authority. Above all, be very careful to avoid brutality or harshness, because you risk creating in them autosuggestions of fear accompanied by hate.

"Furthermore, avoid making damaging or evil remarks about anyone in the presence of children, as often happens in the drawing room, when, without deliberate intention, the nurse or an absent friend is picked to pieces. It follows inevitably that they will imitate your bad example, which may be productive of serious consequences later on."

José Silva says to start teaching your children visualization and imagination when they reach the age of seven. Those, he says, are two faculties of genius.

Coué says, "Awaken in them a desire for knowledge and love of nature, and endeavor to interest them by giving all possible explanations very clearly, in cheerful, good-tempered tones. You must answer their questions pleasantly, instead of checking them roughly with: 'What a bother you are . . . do be quiet . . . you will learn that later,' etc.

"Never, on any account, say to children: 'You are lazy and good-for-nothing,' because, by so doing, you will create in them the very faults which you reproach them with. You should say instead, even if it is not entirely justified by the child's actions: 'You have done much better today than you usually do; well done.' The child will feel flattered by such unaccustomed praise and certainly work much better the next time and, little by little, with proper encouragement, will become an earnest worker.

"Avoid speaking of sickness before children," Coué continued. "Teach them, on the contrary, that health is the normal state, and that sickness is an anomaly, a sort of drawback, that can be avoided by living temperate, well-regulated lives.

"Those who do not bring up their children themselves should be very careful in selecting the people to whom they entrust them. It is not enough that those persons are fond of children; it is necessary that they should also have the very qualities which you desire your children to have," Coué said.

José Silva had an experience like that once. The family was on vacation, and José and Paula left the children with a babysitter while they went out. The children were excited and didn't want to go to bed, so the babysitter told them that there was a monster under the bed that was going to come out and get them and eat them up if they got out of bed.

Children are very imaginative, and if you frighten them by

telling them that there is a monster, they will create one in their imagination. It can be very real to them—so real that they are afraid to get out of bed to go to the bathroom when they need to.

That might have solved the babysitter's problem, but it caused a big problem for the children's parents. It doesn't do any good to tell their children that there isn't actually a monster, because in their mind . . . there is.

José Silva solved the problem using something he had learned during his study of hypnosis: alter the problem in some way, change it from a big problem to a small problem. You may recall that we did that when we talked about changing habits in chapter 7. He did it this way:

He told the children to point their finger at the monster, and every time they would point at the monster and shake their finger at it, the monster would get smaller and smaller and smaller until it was so small that it no longer frightened them. They could then throw it away if they wished.

Coué taught something else that José Silva considered extremely important: "Teach them to love all mankind, without distinction of caste," Coué said. "Teach them that one must be always ready to assist those who are in need of help and never to be afraid of spending time and money on them. That they must, in a word, always think of others rather than only of themselves and that, in acting thus, one feels an inner satisfaction for which the egoist always looks in vain.

"Parents and teachers should make it a point to instruct by example," Coué concluded. "The child is impressionable and open to suggestion. What he sees being done, he will want to do also. Parents should therefore be very careful to set only good examples for their children."

"Suggestions" by Parents

To overcome faults and defects in children and to develop good habits and desirable qualities, Coué had the following suggestion for parents.

"Parents should wait until the child is in bed, and asleep for at least half an hour; then father or mother should noiselessly enter the room, approach the bed, and speak softly to the child about all the things you wish the child to do or to be as regards to health, sleep, work, application, conduct, etc. Then retire as noiselessly as you came, taking great care not to awaken the child.

"This extremely simple proceeding always gives most satisfactory results, and it is easy to understand the reason why it should. When the child sleeps, his body and his conscious being are at rest; his Unconscious self, however, is awake. You speak therefore, to the latter alone and as it is very credulous, it accepts what you say without contradiction and, little by little, the child becomes what the parents desire it to be.

"Let fathers and mothers consider this as a sacred duty to their children. It is mental and moral food, as necessary to them as physical food."

A Mother's Automatic Connection to Her Child

Scientists now know that a mother's ability to communicate with her child is not limited by distance.

A mother has a natural connection—a mental or spiritual connection—with her children. The child was once a part of the mother's body, and a mother retains the ability to communicate with that part of herself, no matter how young or how old, no matter how close or far away the child is. It is automatic.

This is true of animals as well as humans, and has been confirmed by scientific research. A mother rabbit and her baby rabbits were separated by a great distance. The mother was connected to electronic monitoring devices to record her brain-wave activity, and her babies were put to death at random intervals. Later when scientists compared the times, they found that there was a reaction in the mother's brain at the exact instant that each of the baby rabbits was killed.

"The mother has a stronger bond with the child than the father," José Silva said. "It seems like the father reigns in the beta world, the mother reigns in the alpha world. It seems like the male's body grows physically, to deal with physical problems. The mother doesn't grow like that, the mother grows spiritually."

The Soviets proved the bond of mother and offspring in an experiment they conducted with rabbits, he said. Every time they killed a baby rabbit, a memory was registered on the mother rabbit's brain. This happened even from a submarine that was under water, where normal radio signals are blocked. There is some non-physical connection between mother and child.

There have been many stories of mothers who awakened from deep sleep when a child was seriously hurt or killed. This has happened frequently during times of war. It might be several days before the mother receives official notice of her son's death, but she knows.

Mothers can use this ability to help their children. The mother does not need to be a Silva graduate or know how to enter the alpha level in order to do this. Here is how to proceed:

Wait until your child has been asleep for at least half an hour. Then relax, visualize your child (recall what your child looks like), and then you can communicate with your child mentally, on a deep inner level, where the child will not reject your advice and guidance. It doesn't matter how old you child is or how far away, you still have the same subjective (mental) connection for your entire life, even if your child is thousands of miles away.

Whatever you do must be in the child's best interest, something that the child will benefit from doing.

A Problem Solved in Just One Night

José Silva conducted an experiment once many years ago, when he was doing his original research, involving a child who had been wetting the bed his entire life. He asked the child's mother to send her son to another city a hundred and fifty miles away, and to let him stay there with relatives for a full month. Then he told the mother to "program" her child every night, a half hour after his bedtime.

The first night, she closed her eyes and imagined that when her son felt pressure in his tummy and needed to use the bathroom, he would awaken, get up, go to the bathroom, urinate, then go back to bed and go back to sleep. She mentally pictured all of this, like making a "mental movie."

Mr. Silva had cautioned her not to call her son or the relatives he was staying with, because he did not want to contaminate his experiment. But she called anyway, the next day. The relatives were all excited: The boy had not wet the bed that night. And he never wet the bed again.

Identify the behavior that you want to change, and then program your child in this manner. The father can do it too, but in order to do this, the father must know how to enter the alpha level, then activate his mind—become mentally active—and remain at the alpha level while doing his programming.

When there are many problems, try starting with the smallest problem first. When you correct that one, then go to the next most serious problem. If your results are satisfactory, then continue in this same manner. If you are not satisfied with your results starting with the smallest problem, then do just the opposite: Program the most serious problem, the most important one. Think of all the reasons you want to correct this problem, all of the benefits. Think of how many people will benefit in addition to your child and you. The more people who will benefit, the more desire you will have, and this will help you to get much better results.

You can also guide the child to correct the problem. At the age of six, it is easy to teach her to enter the alpha level and help herself. Tell her to relax—first thing in the morning would be a great time. Then go to work on one specific problem. Start with the smallest problem. For instance, if there is something she does that you want her to change—to do differently—then call her attention to the behavior you desire to change. Then tell her to erase that mental picture, and replace it with one doing what you believe would be better for her.

Start by programming her, at night, while she sleeps, as outlined above. You can tell her mentally that you are going to give her a way to do things mentally, so that she will be happier, healthier, and more successful. If you do this with love and desire, then you will get great results.

14

Advanced Technique

*The least you do after learning the Silva System
should be greater than the greatest you did before.*

—José Silva

Information and experiences that you had when you were very young actually influenced the physical growth and development of your brain. This in turn influences the way you think of things and make decisions today. Those early impressions are like ROM in a computer: read-only memory.

They are stored in the part of the brain that functions at 4–7 cycles per second theta brain-wave frequencies. But, as José Silva learned when he studied hypnosis early in his research, you can only function inductively at theta, not deductively.

Inductive reasoning tends to accept things as true. Deductive reasoning involves study and analysis. It is not until we begin to develop the alpha part of the brain—7–14 cycles per second brain frequency—that we begin to develop critical consciousness.

So how are we to neutralize and counteract old negative beliefs and old past traumas if we cannot function deductively at the theta frequencies?

We can do it from neighboring alpha, once we have learned to function deductively at alpha.

We can only function deductively at 20 cycles beta, and at 10 cycles alpha. But 90 percent of people do not maintain the ability to do their thinking at 10 cycles alpha once they pass the age of fourteen. That is why the first thing we do in the Silva Systems is help you learn to enter the alpha brain-wave level and remain there as you activate your mind and learn to function deductively. You learned how to do this in chapter 1.

In order to program while at alpha to neutralize past experiences and correct problems that are rooted at theta, you first need to practice entering the theta level with conscious awareness.

Even though you will not remain at 5 cycles theta once you activate your mind to analyze information and correct problems, your programming will still be effective because you have opened the door to the theta level.

How do you do that? You can do it by continuing to practice the Silva Centering Exercise. With enough repetition you will eventually get there.

Another way is to use a technique called Hand Levitation.

The Hand Levitation Technique

Hand Levitation is a technique that was developed by a world-renowned hypnotist named Milton Erickson. José Silva modified it and included it in the Silva Mind Control course as a way to control pain and speed healing.

You can also learn it to neutralize old traumatic events that you have experienced and negative past programming that might be subconsciously influencing you today.

The Hand Levitation induction technique is a guaranteed way to enter the 5 cycles per second theta brain-wave level, which is where hypnotists do much of their work.

What Kind of Problems Might Be Rooted at Theta?

Limiting belief systems could be rooted at theta.

You see, children function at lower brain frequencies than adults. The overall predominant brain frequency of a five-year-old child will be 5 cycles per second. Impressions are made on the brain at very low frequencies.

If a five-year-old child is told that he is clumsy, or that she is stupid, the child simply accepts that. At that age, the child only reasons inductively, not deductively. The child does not analyze information, but just records it on his or her brain cells.

When you have practiced entering the theta level, then you can enter the alpha level and use the Three-Scenes Technique to program yourself to accomplish your goals, and if the problems—the limiting belief systems—are rooted in theta, your mind can correct them.

There is another reason for opening up the theta levels and bringing them within our reach from the alpha level:

Biological intelligence is rooted at theta. While psychological health problems are rooted at 10 cycles alpha, where human intelligence resides, there are other health problems that are rooted at theta, where biological intelligence resides.

That's why hypnotists are able to use the 5-cycle theta level to prepare patients to have teeth pulled, and even to have surgery, without the use of chemical anesthetics.

You can learn, with practice, to influence biological intelligence.

Your body knows how to heal itself. When you cut your finger, your body knows how to cause the cells to grow back together again.

We are not saying that you will never need a doctor. If it is a big cut, the doctor can sew it up so that there will not be a scar. Antiseptics can be used to keep it from getting infected. But the actual healing is done by your own body.

Doctors are often important—even vital—to the healing process, because they can remove any interference to healing so that nature can take its course. But again, the actual healing process is carried out by your body.

Doctors create an environment that makes it easier for the body to heal. They can keep you alive long enough for the healing to take place.

Now you can help your doctor to help you heal your body.

How does your body know how to heal itself?

Instructions were programmed into your biocomputer brain by whoever originally created and programmed it. Those instructions are part of your biological intelligence. They are automatic. But it is possible, at the correct level, to change those instructions, to take them off of automatic and assume manual control.

The Three-Scenes Technique will be more effective at correcting health problems that are rooted at theta if you continue to practice entering the theta level occasionally, to make sure that there is a clear channel from the alpha part of the brain to the theta part of the brain.

Another benefit of practicing Hand Levitation is that when you have become accustomed to entering the theta level, it will be an easy matter to get to alpha any time you desire.

An Example

One of our students told us that the main reason she took the course is "to heal my child within." She explained, "Basically my child within is terrified of succeeding because anything she did well or succeeded at was always followed by something awful happening, not always necessarily to her but certainly within my family. My father was an extremely violent, psychotic man who spent most of the time beating my mother and my sister."

We advised her that she was not going to correct a problem by dwelling on it. Even "correcting" it is still dealing with the problem—the problem and the solution are just two sides of the same coin.

We don't solve problems by dwelling on them. We move in the direction of our dominant thoughts, so the more time we spend thinking about problems, the stronger they become. Trying to get rid of them is just another way of thinking about them. It is like the old challenge:

It is like somebody telling you: "Don't think of a pink elephant . . . in your bedroom . . . jumping up and down on your bed." How can you *not* think of it? If you don't want to think of a pink elephant, think of something else, bring back a pleasant memory. You can only hold one thought at a time, so make it something you *want* to think about.

In order to neutralize bad memories from the past, you can go to level and visualize what happened back when you were young, then erase it and create a new scenario the way you wish things had happened.

You cannot erase the memory of what happened from your brain neurons. But you can neutralize the old memory with a new memory.

Again, we move in the direction of our dominant thoughts. So whether you are thinking of the abuse, or of the alternative to the abuse—you are still paying attention to the problem . . . the abuse.

What you need to do is program what you want in your life today.

Remember the things we have talked about, like Juan Silva's advice on how to increase your desire and motivation in chapter 11.

Remember the Laws of Programming in chapter 10. Also remember that just thinking about something isn't enough, you also need to take action in the physical world.

Consider going to a Boys or Girls Club in a neighborhood where they don't have a lot of money. Go in and volunteer your services to brighten the place up and create an environment that inspires the kids and makes them feel good about themselves. Have the kids go with you to companies that have excess inventory that they can donate to the effort. The kids can hold fund raisers to buy what they can't get donated.

Get the kids and the parents and the whole neighborhood involved in the project; let them all play a part. Then everybody will feel good and will be proud of what they have done.

And guess what:

That will do more than anything else to motivate your inner child. The best way to improve self-confidence and self-esteem and to develop a better personality and become more popular is to take part in constructive and creative activities to make the world a better place to live, and to do it because we are part of humanity and it is part of our responsibility.

This has proven to be so powerful that we include that line in the headers of our websites: *Leave behind a better world for those who follow.*

Humanity is like a team; life is like a team sport. Some individuals have more talent than others, and some get more recognition and rewards than others, but ultimately we all win or lose together, as a team.

Don't just talk about feeling safe to be visible and successful; go out and demonstrate it.

If you are hesitant to take the first step, then go to level and program to take that first step.

The value of learning to go to the theta level with conscious awareness (as you do when you use Hand Levitation) is that it opens the door to those levels, where those old memories are stored.

Then when you program yourself at alpha, the images of the work you are doing and the people who are benefiting (remember to "program in the future in a past-tense sense") will feel great to the "inner child" and you will do just fine.

You can program the total project, picture the end result as a done deal, accomplished.

Then program each step as you prepare to do it.

Take Action to Make Things Happen

Nothing happens until you take action. Juan Silva had a great story about that too.

He was sitting and meditating on how he could go about inventing something, when his stepfather came in and pulled him up out of the chair and pushed him towards the shop and told him to get to work.

Juan put a rod on a lathe and started turning it, for no reason other than to be doing something. He noticed that he was creating a rack gear, and as he looked at it, the idea came to him that a rack gear would be a great way to handle the problem of all of the different size coins used in Mexico, and how to accommodate them in a vending machine.

That invention earned him a lot of money. But it didn't come from sitting and meditating on it—it came when he got up and started doing something. Even though he didn't have any specific purpose in mind, just the fact that he got his body into action made the difference.

As he said, when you start moving around, then there is a better chance that the solution will bump into you.

How to Practice Hand Levitation

Hand Levitation will take you to the theta level with conscious awareness. We are not able to function inductive at theta—only deductively—but when you have opened the door to the theta level, then the programming you do at alpha will reach into theta and correct problems that are rooted there.

Hand Levitation guarantees that you will enter deep levels of mind and low brain frequencies, all the way to the theta brainwave level.

Entering level with Hand Levitation is very simple, although it may take you a few minutes to do it in the beginning. The technique was originally developed by Milton Erickson so that his patients could take themselves to level and he would not have to spend as much of his time guiding them there.

Mr. Silva modified the technique to suit our purposes. Here's how it works:

You start this exercise sitting upright in a chair, with both hands resting in your lap, palms down.

You start at your stronger hand—your dominant hand. If you are right-handed, this means your right hand.

Your goal is to use your imagination to cause your hand to rise from your lap all by itself. You imagine it rising up to touch your face—without any conscious effort on your part.

The subconscious—which you have already converted into an inner conscious level—causes it to rise, at the direction of your imagination.

When your hand comes up "all by itself," this confirms that you are at your correct level. It confirms that you have lowered your brain frequency all the way to 5 cycles theta.

You are raising your hand with your inner conscious thoughts, not with outer conscious thought and effort.

Concentrating on a single thing is one of the most common ways to get into a meditative state. When you concentrate totally on your hand, and exclude everything else, your brain—which will be totally bored—will slow down to the theta frequencies, 5 cycles per second. Your concentration actually causes you to enter your level.

When you begin, assume an erect sitting position, allowing yourself enough room to raise your arm comfortably. Then look at and concentrate on your stronger hand, while both hands rest on your lap, palms down. Look at your stronger hand. Keep your eyes focused on your hand.

Cause your hand to feel sensitive, very sensitive. Slowly cause one finger to move, then cause your fingers to separate from one another and at the same time cause your hand to rise from your lap.

Continue to allow your hand to rise in the direction of your face. Feel your arm becoming lighter and lighter as the back of your hand draws closer and closer to your face. Your hand may feel as though a balloon is lifting it.

Allow your hand and arm to become still lighter and lighter as you continue to help them rise higher and higher.

When the back of your hand touches your face, close your eyes, take a deep breath, and while exhaling, return your hand to its resting position on your lap.

You may use Hand Levitation to enter deeper, healthier programming levels. Remember: every time you practice Hand Levitation, you will enter deeper healthier levels of mind.

When your hand comes up by itself, this removes all doubt and confirms that you have indeed entered your level—the theta level.

It might take some people as long as an hour for this to work, so recall the suggestions we have made: Before you begin, enter the alpha level and think of all of the reasons you have for learning this technique. Think of all of the people who will benefit when you are able to solve more problems, when you are no longer plagued by problems of the distant past and are functioning more confidently and effectively.

The more people who will benefit, the greater your desire will be. The more desire you have, the easier it will be to master Hand Levitation.

These are additional tools that you can use. As always, the choice is yours. You can choose to watch television, or you can choose to practice. If you are serious about solving problems and achieving the success you desire, you know what to do.

You only need to make one choice at a time. You can do whatever you want to do tomorrow. So . . . what are you going to do today? Are you going to make that one choice today and learn a technique that can help you achieve greater success? I hope so.

José Silva has his own unique way of explaining his research findings. Let's listen in as he talks to Silva lecturers and lecturer candidates during an instructor training session in Laredo.

José Silva Discusses His Research

Now you can eventually go to theta with the Silva Centering Exercise, until you finally get there. But when you get to theta, you cannot activate your mind there.

But if you have to work on a problem, and it's rooted in theta, when you activate your mind you come to alpha to correct it, it works because now you know where theta is and you've been there before.

But if you've never been into theta before, there is no way you can correct problems from alpha, into theta. But once you get to theta, and know where it's at, then you can correct problems in theta also, from alpha. Alpha is the only place where you can activate your mind, other than beta.

There are thousands, some say, of mental dimensions. How many levels there are . . . an infinite number.

We say that a problem starts under certain conditions when your mind is at a specific level. And to be able to correct it, we must go to the same level, in order for it to be within our reach, to be able to correct it. If it is beyond our reach, we couldn't correct it.

So mind, looking for that problem, has to go deep enough, to where it originated.

So the hand comes up by itself, when you desire for it to come up, it comes up automatically. But you need to be at theta for it to come up automatically. At first you help it to get there, then it becomes automatic.

So when it rises on its own, that is proof that you have reached theta for sure.

It is believed that 10 percent of health problems are rooted at beta. 80 percent at alpha. And 10 percent in theta.

Psychological problems, functional problems, can be at beta or alpha. They eventually become organic, then they are rooted in theta.

Influencing the Body's Healing Mechanism

I was testing this individual at one time, for positive hallucination. I had a piece of stainless steel, which I held with a pair of pliers. The individual should feel it as red-hot. That is called "positive hallucination." The subject detects more than what's there. Red-hot. When I touched him, he screamed. He felt the burn. He felt the heat. That is positive hallucination. He was sensing more than what was there.

Ninety percent of subjects you do this to develop a little red spot, little red dot, as if they were burned with boiling water, or something like that. Ten percent develop a blister. I was lucky to see that phenomenon. My subject developed a blister.

I said, "What happened here?" I didn't burn him. Did I fool the healing process, the natural healing process of the body, to send healing chemistry to a spot that did not need it? Sure. Build a blister, build new skin under it, and get rid of that burned skin. But it's not burned.

Then I figured, could we send in extra healing chemistry to accelerate the healing process? Of course you can do that. If you can do one, you can do the other. No question there.

So, so many things came through in experimenting with hypnosis. But then I found that the deeper a person went, the more they forgot. At a certain level, they start forgetting. If you want them to forget everything, then you suggest to them that they forget everything. If you don't want them to forget, then you tell them to remember everything, and they will.

But you leave it alone, the deeper they go, the more they forget, until they forget everything. They remember nothing. If you want them to remember, you have to tell them to remember, then they will. But naturally, they won't.

We kept on working with them hour after hour after hour after hour after hour, and so forth and so on, until finally they started remembering a little bit. Like they did before (earlier in their training). Then more hours, and they start remembering more, and more, and more, as though they had dreamed, and so forth, until finally they remember everything.

We wanted a level where they could remember everything. Not like in hypnosis. So we found that what was happening, they were coming up from theta to alpha. Theta is the deepest you can go in hypnosis. They were coming a little bit at a time, until finally they got to alpha, and then remembered everything, they could talk to you and everything, like they did before.

A hypnotized subject in theta never asked questions. Their mind functions inductively, like when they were prior to seven years of age. You take them to 5 cycles theta; that is comparable to when they were five years old.

Why do they forget? Because now they are fifty. That happened forty-five years ago, how can they remember? So there at five, their mind functioning inductively, they cannot formulate a question. They can answer questions, but they can never ask questions, because they are not able to.

So we found out at what level we can become active. That's how we discovered the alpha dimension.

15
Leadership

Success is not for the timid. It is for those who seek guidance,
make decisions, and take decisive action.

—JOSÉ SILVA

You now have in your possession one of the best and most complete collections of techniques ever assembled to help you boost your self-confidence, eliminate fears and phobias, become a more powerful communicator, improve your ability to influence yourself and others, develop your brain power, and be a leader who inspires people to take part in constructive and creative activities to make the world a better place to live.

It is now in your hands to build a better future. To do that takes both mental *and* physical action.

Everything begins with a thought, but thought without action doesn't solve problems. Action without thought causes more problems than it solves. We need both, and that is exactly what we do.

Some people seem to think that there is some magical way that just thinking about something will somehow cause it to manifest in the physical world. It doesn't work that way. We were each given a physical body to use to convert our ideas into physical reality.

José Silva put it this way: "Being a collector of insights is not sufficient; utilizing insights for the betterment of self and humanity are more worthwhile projects."

Tips to Help You Succeed

You can use the following suggestions as a playbook to guide you in selecting and applying the various techniques to help yourself and others.

First, a couple of things that are important to keep in mind.

We advise people to learn the techniques the way José Silva taught them. Once you are having success with them, you have a baseline" to work with.

After you know what to expect from the technique the way he designed it, then you can try changing it if you think it will help. You can compare the results you get with your modified technique with the results you got with his version. If the results are better, then you know that you have something that works well for you.

That is why we advise people not to mix any other technique or system—no matter how well it works for them—until they have gotten some results from our System, so that they can compare and see what works best.

Xue Kuiyang, our Silva UltraMind director in China, put it this way: "The Silva System is the foundation to upgrade any learnings. My experience is that Silva techniques make my tra-ditional Chinese medicine practice, including acupuncture, massage, Taiji and Qigong, totally intuitive. No thinking is necessary. Just automatically download the therapy. Quite amazing. More interesting," she added, "is that I have learned dancing, drawing, and other skills by myself."

One way that some people try to modify our System is to use music to help them relax. The problem is that music has fluctuating frequencies, so while it might be relaxing, it won't help you to enter and stay at the 10 cycles per second alpha brain-wave level. That is why we use the Alpha Sound, which taps 10 times per second. The brain will respond to teach tap, and this will help to guide it to remain at the alpha level.

The Theta Sound also seems to work well, and many people like it more than the Alpha Sound. The Theta Sound is 5 cycles per second, the first subharmonic of the alpha frequency. You can hear a sample of these at www.SilvaNow.com and purchase them from our www.SilvaCourses.com website if you wish.

If some merchant claims that their music or their "brainwave entrainment" sounds help you enter an altered state of consciousness, or help with any medical condition, then ask for research that was conducted in a scientific manner: double-blind (nobody knows if they are getting the real thing or a placebo) so that expectations don't influence the outcome.

Scientific method also requires objective feedback and replication—tangible results that anyone can see, and the ability to confirm the results by repeating the experiment with different subjects.

A lot of people point to anecdotal reports from individuals who feel that something has helped them. That is not scientific research. There are always a few people who will respond the way they are expected to, even if there is no reason to. That is how placebos work.

It is not necessary to use the Alpha Sound in order to get all of the results and benefits of the Silva techniques. The Alpha Sound can make it easier to learn. But it doesn't do the work for you—you still need to do the work yourself.

The best advice is to do whatever solves problems—creates tangible, physical improvement—while not causing any harm.

Remember That Mental Pictures Influence People

When you are interacting with someone in their presence—within range of the physical part of the body's aura (approximately eight meters)—remember to visualize the desired outcome. Create a mental picture of the solution you desire, and confidently *expect* it to happen. This is covered in detail in chapter 12.

When you know that you will be interacting with someone, you can program ahead of time with the Three-Scenes Technique, which you learned in chapter 4. Then, when you are with that person, visualize (recall) the images you created in the second and third scenes.

Here is how you can remain at the alpha level with your eyes open while visualizing the images: Do not look at anything directly, but "defocus" your vision. It is as if you are daydreaming: you can be aware of your physical surroundings indirectly, while being aware of your mental pictures directly.

You can also learn to mentally influence people at a distance, but that is beyond the scope of this book. The book *Silva UltraMind Systems ESP for Business Success* covers this in detail, and includes José Silva's actual ESP training. You can also learn in a live seminar, online training, or home study. For information please visit www.SilvaCourses.com.

The Importance of Practice and Purpose

Two of the most important keys to success with the Silva techniques are:

1. Practice. Get in the habit of going to level every day. For help and guidance, be sure to read the information in the "Guidance for Grads" section of the www.SIGA.org website.
2. Purpose. Juan Silva always emphasized the importance of reinforcing your reasons for using the Silva techniques.

Before going to level, Juan reminds us, think about *why* this is valuable to you. Especially think about how many people who will benefit. The more people who benefit, the better. We wrote about his approach to boosting enthusiasm for your desire in chapter 11.

José Silva reminded us frequently that the Creator did not give us this wonderful brain and wonderful mind just to play with for our own amusement. They were given to us for a purpose, and that purpose is to correct problems.

In order to qualify for help from higher intelligence, José Silva said, you must correct problems. The more problems you correct, and the more people who benefit, the more help you will qualify for.

"A human is not one who looks like one," he used to tell us, "it is one who acts like one."

You can read more of his thoughts on this in chapters 9 and 10.

Small Steps Equal Big Success

It is natural to be eager to be very successful very quickly. That is often not the best way. José Silva explained it this way:

"Some people are destroyed by their first failure, while others are destroyed by their first major success. So let's have successes in small amounts, leading up to being able to be successful."

For twenty years, José Silva wrote a "From the Founder" column in every issue of the *Silva Mind Control Newsletter*. Here is one of his favorites, and it is just as relevant today as it was when he wrote it back in 1980:

My brother Juan and I were giving out the awards to the Silva lecturers during the recently completed Silva International Convention and, as is usually the case, all eyes were on us and the winners who came to center stage for their awards.

In the midst of the applause and cheers that the winners received as their names were called out, I became very reflective.

"Why," I asked myself, "are these people getting an award? What made them special in this particular regard this year?"

Becoming conscious of those thoughts, I began to seek a strand that connected all the winners this year. Was there a link to their performances? Did they share something in common?

We are blessed, I think, in having outstanding individuals associated with us as lecturers and graduates, and this fact is a principal reason why the Silva System has become one of the most significant planetary forces in existence today. It is these people—all of them—that give life to our work, and it is their zeal that has carried it to almost every corner of the world.

Yet, for this particular year, there were some who had excelled even further. Why?

As I kept thinking of this, that connecting strand eventually appeared. These graduates, it seemed, had been specially careful to notice small details.

All of us focus on the bigger things—and well we should. But oftentimes, the small details do not get the attention they deserve. After all, big things are nothing more than the accumulation of small things. It stands to reason, therefore, that small details make big things happen.

This is not as philosophical as it may sound, for the person who does small things well, regardless of the importance, is going to do big things well. Conversely, the person who does not give importance to small things is not going to make big things happen.

In our work, we have fully become aware of this, and we attempt to better ourselves through the very powerful tool of habit. Individuals are creatures of habit, and if we program ourselves to good habits, we shall, indeed, become "better and better." But the opposite can also be true. Nourishing bad habits will become disastrous to the individual.

Making it a habit to do small things well day in and day out, regardless of how insignificant they may seem, will eventually program us to do big things well. This programming, I felt, was what the winners had in common. The small things had given them their prize.

One of the most useful tools our System has, I think, is that it allows each of us to assume responsibility for our total self, and to allow each of us to analyze our total being through the different parts that make each of us a unique human being.

Our human system is made up of many parts, each one playing a definite but distinct role. All of them are equal, and the ability to blend all of their functions harmoniously is a main task of the Silva System.

Through our System, we are provided an effective way to search for self, but once we do that we must assume total responsibility for ourselves, including each and every part of our being and each and every role that we as humans play.

Our journey as humans on this planet is comprised of many decisions, many alternatives, many opportunities, many disillusions, many joys, and many sorrows. All of these situations will shape us as human beings, and they will affect our way of life and our way of being. They are significant events in our lives, yet if we look closely we can notice that all of these situations came about because of small things.

That big opportunity arrived in my own life, but it came about because day by day I paid attention to doing my job well, learning as much as I could, possessing a cheerful personality, coping with the stresses and responsibilities of the job.

Yes, we must indeed have our sights fixed on the big events in our lives; but we must never forget those small things.

It was doing small things well that earned those individuals their awards this year, and, in a bigger framework, it is doing small things well that eventually will make us better and better human beings.

Cooperation and Organized Effort

Scientists study biological systems and how they evolve in order to learn why some survive while most become extinct. They have discovered something that should be obvious: groups working together have an advantage over individuals who just look out for themselves.

Animals who live in societies where there is a lot of cooperation and some division of labor, such as ants, bees, wasps, and humans, have taken over the earth. We have all seen how all of the members of a colony of ants work together for a common cause, and how closely bees and wasps live together in their hives.

Now, scientists tell us, ants, bees, and wasps take up most of the insect biomass—the sheer weight of insects.

While insects may be operating on instincts that are reinforced genetically by the evolutionary process, humans have something else that encourages them to turn to religion and spirituality in their search for the best way to proceed:

Humans have a spiritual factor.

What Makes Humans Different

Animals, and even plants, have an objective factor, and a subjective factor.

Humans have those, but they also have a spiritual factor.

The spiritual factor prompts humans to ask questions like, "If I am only for myself, then why should anyone else be for me?"

Napoleon Hill, author of *Think and Grow Rich*, wrote about how the richest and most successful people in the world used organized effort to accomplish far more than they could accomplish on their own. They used organized effort objectively in their businesses, and also subjectively with a technique he called *mastermind*.

José Silva said that we are all in the same boat, and if the boat sinks, we all go.

Steve Jobs and Steve Wozniak became best friends immediately when their mutual friend, Bill Fernandez, introduced them to each other in 1971. They complemented each other perfectly:

Jobs was a charismatic salesman, while The Woz was an engineer who loved to solve complex technical problems. They needed each other, and their organized effort produced Apple Computer and changed the world.

Followers and Leaders

Jobs said that Apple Computer was "product-driven," not "market-driven." When someone told him that he needed to give people what they wanted, Jobs replied, "They don't know what they want until we show it to them."

José Silva was the same way. He invested twenty-two years of his life and $500,000 of his own money to develop his "product."

He got it right: millions of people worldwide have learned about his course by word of mouth, without any advertising campaigns or celebrity spokesmen.

We are following his example. While other companies send out compelling advertising messages about how much you can benefit from this week's new best-ever product, we continue to support the System that José Silva developed.

We might not always tell you what you want to hear, but we will always tell you what is right and what works best.

Your Playbook: To Become Confident, Influential, and Successful

When you first wake up, go to the bathroom, etc., then enter your level and pre-program the day. Mentally picture yourself making good decisions and succeeding at solving problems.

Perform a small act of kindness every day.

Practice the Silva Centering Exercise at least once a week.

Every week do at least one thing for somebody else, preferably without their knowledge, that you cannot be reimbursed or compensated for.

Use your level to analyze information and make decisions.

Use the Three-Scenes Technique and Mental Rehearsal as needed to prepare yourself to take action to solve problems.

Enter your level and program to neutralize any impediments that may be holding you back.

Take action in the physical world.

Before you go to sleep, use the MentalVideo to prepare a report for higher intelligence about what you are doing to solve problems and improve living conditions on the planet. Let your tutor know that you are doing the work, and you are open to guidance if they have a better way. If you are having trouble with a project, include this in your MentalVideo and ask for help—but only if you are stuck and don't know how to proceed.

Memorize the spiritual statement that José Silva considered so important that he included it at the end of the final conditioning cycle of the day in every class, and repeat it just before going to sleep:

I will continue to strive to take part in constructive and creative activities to make the world a better place to live, so that when I move on, I shall have left behind a better world for those who follow. I will consider the whole of humanity, depending on their ages, as fathers or mothers, brothers or sisters, sons or daughters. I am a superior human being, I have greater understanding, compassion, and patience with others.

Now It Is Your Turn to Be a Leader

You have now learned how to function with conscious awareness at the alpha level, and can use this inner conscious level to help you in all areas of your life:

You can communicate subjectively (mentally) with your body to keep it healthy.

You can communicate subjectively with other people to resolve conflicts and solve problems more effectively.

You can communicate subjectively with higher intelligence and obtain guidance to help correct abnormalities and make the world a better place to live.

As José Silva used to say: it has been a pleasure working for you and with you, and please feel free to call on us any time we can be of service.

The future is now up to you, so take action, take every opportunity to apply what you have learned, and make the rest of your life the *best* of your life.

Thank you.

Appendix A

The Silva Centering Exercise by José Silva

The Silva Centering Exercise helps you discover an inner dimension, a dimension that you can use to become healthier, luckier, and more successful in achieving your goals.

When you learn to function from this inner dimension, you automatically become more spiritual, more human, healthier, safer from accidents, and a more successful problem solver.

In order for you to use this inner dimension, you need to hear the Silva Centering Exercise a total of ten hours, and to follow the simple directions in the mind exercise.

How to Read the Silva Centering Exercise

When reading the Silva Centering Exercise, read in a relaxed, natural voice. Be close enough so that the listener can hear you comfortably. Read loud enough to be heard, and read as though you were reading to a seven-year-old child. Speak each word clearly and distinctly.

Have the listener assume a comfortable position. A sitting position is preferred, but the most important thing is to make sure the listener is comfortable. If uncomfortable, the listener will not relax as much and will not get as much benefit from the exercise.

Avoid distractions, such as loud outside noises. There should be enough light so you can read comfortably, but not extremely bright lights.

If the person shows any signs of nervousness or appears to be uncomfortable, stop reading, tell them to relax and make themselves comfortable. When they are comfortable and ready, then continue.

Take your time when you read; there is no need to rush.

Note: Do not read the headings (in bold print). They are for your information.

The Silva Centering Exercise

DEEPENING (PHYSICAL RELAXATION AT LEVEL 3)

Find a comfortable position, close your eyes, take a deep breath and while exhaling, mentally repeat and visualize the number 3 three times. (pause)

To help you learn to relax physically at level 3, I am going to direct your attention to different parts of your body.

Concentrate your sense of awareness on your scalp, the skin that covers your head; you will detect a fine vibration, a tingling sensation, a feeling of warmth caused by circulation. (pause) Now release and completely relax all tensions and ligament pressures from this part of your head and place it in a deep state of relaxation that will grow deeper as we continue. (pause)

Concentrate your sense of awareness on your forehead, the skin that covers your forehead; you will detect a fine vibration, a tingling sensation, a feeling of warmth caused by circulation. (pause) Now release and completely relax all tensions and ligament pressures from this part of your head and place it in a deep state of relaxation that will grow deeper as we continue. (pause)

Concentrate your sense of awareness on your eyelids and the tissue surrounding your eyes; you will detect a fine vibration, a tingling sensation, a feeling of warmth caused by circulation. (pause) Now release and completely relax all tensions and ligament pressures from this part of your head and place it in a deep state of relaxation that will grow deeper as we continue. (pause)

Concentrate your sense of awareness on your face, the skin covering your cheeks; you will detect a fine vibration, a tingling sensation, a feeling of warmth caused by circulation. (pause) Now release and completely relax all tensions and ligament pressures from this part of your head and place it in a deep state of relaxation that will grow deeper as we continue. (pause)

Concentrate on the outer portion of your throat, the skin covering your throat area; you will detect a fine vibration, a tingling sensation, a feeling of warmth caused by circulation. (pause) Now release and completely relax all tensions and ligament pressures from this part of your body and place it in a deep state of relaxation that will grow deeper as we continue. (pause)

Concentrate within the throat area and relax all tensions and ligament pressures from this part of your body and place it in a deep state of relaxation, going deeper and deeper every time. (pause)

Concentrate on your shoulders; feel your clothing in contact with your body. (pause) Feel the skin and the vibration of the skin covering this part of your body. (pause) Relax all tensions and ligament pressures and place your shoulders in a deep state of relaxation, going deeper and deeper every time. (pause)

Concentrate on your chest; feel your clothing in contact with this part of your body. (pause) Feel the skin and the vibration of your skin covering your chest. (pause) Relax all tensions and ligament pressures and place your chest in a deep state of relaxation, going deeper and deeper every time. (pause)

Concentrate within the chest area; relax all organs; relax all glands; relax all tissues, including the cells themselves, and cause them to function in a rhythmic, healthy manner. (pause)

Concentrate on your abdomen; feel the clothing in contact with this part of your body. (pause) Feel the skin and the vibration of your skin covering your abdomen. (pause) Relax all tensions and ligament pressures and place your abdomen in a deep state of relaxation, going deeper and deeper every time. (pause)

Concentrate within the abdominal area; relax all organs; relax all glands; relax all tissues, including the cells themselves and cause them to function in a rhythmic, healthy manner. (pause)

Concentrate on your thighs; feel your clothing in contact with this part of your body. (pause) Feel the skin and the vibration of your skin covering your thighs. (pause) Relax all tensions and ligament pressures and place your thighs in a deep state of relaxation, going deeper and deeper every time. (pause)

Sense the vibrations at the bones within the thighs; by now these vibrations should be easily detectable. (pause)

Concentrate on your knees; feel the skin and the vibration of your skin covering the knees. (pause) Relax all tensions and ligament pressures and place your knees in a deep state of relaxation, going deeper and deeper every time (pause)

Concentrate on your calves; feel the skin and the vibration of the skin covering your calves. (pause) Relax all tensions and ligament pressures and place these parts of your body in a deep state of relaxation, going deeper and deeper every time. (pause)

To enter a deeper, healthier level of mind, concentrate on your toes. (pause) Enter a deeper, healthier level of mind.

To enter a deeper, healthier level of mind, concentrate on the soles of your feet. (pause) Enter a deeper, healthier level of mind. (pause)

To enter a deeper, healthier level of mind, concentrate on the heels of your feet. (pause) Enter a deeper, healthier level of mind. (pause)

Now cause your feet to feel as though they do not belong to your body. (pause)

Feel your feet as though they do not belong to your body. (pause)

Your feet feel as though they do not belong to your body. (pause)

Your feet, ankles, calves, and knees feel as though they do not belong to your body. (pause)

Your feet, ankles, calves, knees, thighs, waist, shoulders, arms, and hands feel as though they do not belong to your body. (pause)

You are now at a deeper, healthier level of mind, deeper than before.

This is your physical relaxation level 3. Whenever you mentally repeat and visualize the number 3, your body will relax as completely as you are now, and more so every time you practice.

DEEPENING (MENTAL RELAXATION AT LEVEL 2)

To enter the mental relaxation level 2, mentally repeat and visualize the number 2 several times, and you are at level 2, a deeper level than 3. (pause) Level 2 is for mental relaxation, where noises will not distract you. Instead, noises will help you to relax mentally more and more.

To help you learn to relax mentally at level 2, I am going to call your attention to different passive scenes. Visualizing any scene that makes you tranquil and passive will help you relax mentally.

Your being at the beach on a nice summer day may be a tranquil and passive scene for you. (pause)

A day out fishing may be a tranquil and passive scene for you. (pause)

A tranquil and passive scene for you may be a walk through the woods on a beautiful summer day, when the breeze is just right, where there are tall shade trees, beautiful flowers, a very blue sky, an occasional white cloud, birds singing in the distance, even squirrels playing on the tree limbs. Hear birds singing in the distance. (pause)

This is mental relaxation level 2, where noises will not distract you.

To enhance mental relaxation at level 2, practice visualizing tranquil and passive scenes.

TO ENTER YOUR CENTER

To enter level 1, mentally repeat and visualize the number 1 several times. (pause)

You are now at level 1, the basic level where you can function from your center.

DEEPENING EXERCISES

To enter deeper, healthier levels of mind, practice with the count-down deepening exercises.

To deepen, count downward from 25 to 1, or from 50 to 1, or from 100 to 1. When you reach the count of 1, you will have reached a deeper, healthier level of mind, deeper than before.

You will always have full control and complete dominion over your faculties and senses at all levels of the mind including the outer conscious level.

WHEN TO PRACTICE

The best time to practice the countdown deepening exercises is in the morning when you wake up. Remain in bed at least five minutes practicing the countdown deepening exercises.

The second best time to practice is at night, when you are ready to retire.

The third best time to practice is at noon after lunch.

Five minutes of practice is good; ten minutes is very good; fifteen minutes is excellent.

To practice once a day is good; two times a day is very good; and three times a day is excellent.

If you have a health problem, practice for fifteen minutes, three times a day.

TO COME OUT OF LEVELS

To come out of any level of the mind, count to yourself mentally from 1 to 5 and tell yourself that at the count of 5 you will open your eyes, be wide awake, feeling fine and in perfect health, feeling better than before.

Then proceed to count slowly from 1 to 2, then to 3, and at the count of 3 mentally remind yourself that at the count of 5 you will open your eyes, be wide awake, feeling fine and in prefect health, feeling better than before.

Proceed to count slowly to 4, then to 5. At the count of 5 and with your eyes open, mentally tell yourself, "I am wide awake, feeling fine, and in perfect health, feeling better than before. And this is so."

DEEPENING (ROUTINE CYCLE)

To help you enter a deeper, healthier level of mind, I am going to count from 10 to 1. On each descending number, you will feel yourself going deeper and you will enter a deeper, healthier level of mind.

10 – 9, feel going deeper,

8 – 7 – 6, deeper and deeper

5 – 4 – 3, deeper and deeper,

2 – 1

You are now at a deeper, healthier level of mind, deeper than before.

You may enter a deeper, healthier level of mind by simply relaxing your eyelids. Relax your eyelids. (pause) Feel how relaxed they are. (pause) Allow this feeling of relaxation to flow slowly downward throughout your body, all the way down to your toes. (pause)

It is a wonderful feeling to be deeply relaxed, a very healthy state of being.

To help you enter a deeper, healthier level of mind, I am going to count from 1 to 3. At that moment, you will project yourself mentally to your ideal place of relaxation. I will then stop talking to you, and when you next hear my voice, one hour of time will have elapsed at this level of mind. My voice will not startle you; you will take a deep breath, relax, and go deeper.

1 – (pause) – 2 – (pause) – 3. Project yourself mentally to your ideal place of relaxation until you hear my voice again. Relax. (Lecturer: remain silent for about thirty seconds.)

Relax. (pause) Take a deep breath and as you exhale, relax and go deeper. (pause)

RAPPORT

You will continue to listen to my voice; you will continue to follow the instructions at this level of the mind and any other level, including the outer conscious level. This is for your benefit; you desire it, and it is so.

Whenever you hear me mention the word "Relax," all unnecessary movements and activities of your body, brain, and mind will cease immediately, and you will become completely passive and relaxed physically and mentally.

I may bring you out of this level or a deeper level than this by counting to you from 1 to 5. At the count of 5, your eyes will open; you will be wide awake, feeling fine and in perfect health.

I may bring you out of this level or a deeper level than this by touching your left shoulder three times. When you feel my hand touch your left shoulder for the third time, your eyes will open; you will be wide awake, feeling fine and in perfect health. And this is so.

GENIUS STATEMENTS

The difference between genius mentality and lay mentality is that geniuses use more of their minds and use them in a special manner.

You are now learning to use more of your mind and to use it in a special manner.

BENEFICIAL STATEMENTS

The following are beneficial statements that you may occasionally repeat while at these levels of the mind. Repeat mentally after me. (Lecturer: read slowly.)

My increasing mental faculties are for serving humanity better.

Every day, in every way, I am getting better, better, and better.

Positive thoughts bring me benefits and advantages I desire.

I have full control and complete dominion over my sensing faculties at this level of the mind and any other level, including the outer conscious level. And this is so.

I will always maintain a perfectly healthy body and mind.

EFFECTIVE SENSORY PROJECTION STATEMENTS

Effective Sensory Projection statements for success.

I am now learning to attune my intelligence by developing my sensing faculties and to project them to any problem area so as to be aware of any actions taking place, if this is necessary and beneficial for humanity.

I am now learning to correct any problems I detect.

Negative thoughts and negative suggestions have no influence over me at any level of the mind.

POST EFFECTS: PREVIEW OF NEXT SESSION

You have practiced entering deep, healthy levels of mind. In your next session, you will enter a deeper, healthier level of mind, faster and easier than this time.

POST EFFECTS: STANDARD

Every time you function at these levels of the mind, you will receive beneficial effects physically and mentally.

You may use these levels of the mind to help yourself physically and mentally.

You may use these levels of the mind to help your loved ones, physically and mentally.

You may use these levels of the mind to help any human being who needs help, physically and mentally.

You will never use these levels of the mind to harm any human being; if this be your intention, you will not be able to function within these levels of the mind.

You will always use these levels of the mind in a constructive, creative manner for all that is good, honest, pure, clean, and positive. And this is so.

You will continue to strive to take part in constructive and creative activities to make this a better world to live in, so that when we move on, we shall have left behind a better world for those who follow. You will consider the whole of humanity, depending on their ages, as fathers or mothers, brothers or sisters, sons or daughters. You are a superior human being; you have greater understanding, compassion, and patience with others.

BRING OUT

In a moment, I am going to count from 1 to 5. At that moment, you will open your eyes, be wide awake, feeling fine and in perfect health, feeling better than before. You will have no ill effects whatsoever in your head, no headache; no ill effects whatsoever in your hearing, no buzzing in your ears; no ill effects whatsoever in your vision and eyesight; vision, eyesight, and hearing improve every time you function at these levels of mind.

1 – 2, coming out slowly now.

3, at the count of 5, you will open your eyes, be wide awake, feeling fine and in perfect health, feeling better than before, feeling the way you feel when you have slept the right amount of revitalizing, refreshing, relaxing, healthy sleep.

4 – 5, eyes open, wide awake, feeling fine and in perfect health, feeling better than before.

(Reader: Be sure to observe whether or not the person is wide awake. If in doubt, touch the person's left shoulder three times and while doing so say: "Wide awake, feeling fine and in perfect health. And this is so.")

It is recommended that everyone practice staying at their center for fifteen minutes a day to normalize all abnormal conditions of the body and mind.

Appendix B

Alternative Ways to Find the Alpha Level

Note: It is not necessary to do this if you are learning by having someone read the Silva Centering Exercise to you, or are using a recording of the Silva Centering Exercise.

I will give you a simple way to relax, and you will do better and better at this as you practice.

I will also give you a Beneficial Statement to help you.

This is how you train your mind. You relax, lower your brain frequency to the alpha level, and practice using imagination and visualization.

Because you cannot read this book and relax simultaneously, it is necessary that you read the instructions first, so that you can put the book down, close your eyes, and follow them.

Here they are:

1. Sit comfortably in a chair and close your eyes. Any position that is comfortable is a good position.
2. Take a deep breath, and as you exhale, relax your body.
3. Count backward slowly from 50 to 1.

4. Daydream about some peaceful place you know.

5. Say to yourself mentally, "Every day, in every way, I am getting better, better, and better."

6. Remind yourself mentally that when you open your eyes at the count of 5, you will feel wide awake, better than before. When you reach the count of 3, repeat this, and when you open your eyes, repeat it ("I am wide awake, feeling better than before").

You already know steps one and two. You do them daily when you get home in the evening. Add a countdown, a peaceful scene, and a beneficial statement to help you become better and better, and you are ready for a final count-out.

Read the instructions once more. Then put the book down and do it.

Learning to Function Consciously at the Alpha Level

As stated previously, you learn to enter the alpha level and function there with just one day of training when you attend the Silva UltraMind ESP Systems live training programs. You can use the audio recordings to learn to enter the alpha level within a few days with either a Silva home-study program or the free lessons at the www.SilvaNow.com website. You can also record the Silva Centering Exercise in appendix A and listen to it, or have someone read it to you.

If you have already learned to enter the alpha level by one of those methods, you can skip the following instructions for practicing countdown deepening exercises for the next forty days.

If not, then follow these instructions from José Silva:

When you enter sleep, you enter alpha. But you quickly go right through alpha to the deeper levels of theta and delta.

Throughout the night, your brain moves back and forth through alpha, theta, and delta, like the ebb and flow of the tide. These cycles last about ninety minutes.

In the morning, as you exit sleep, you come out through alpha, back into the faster beta frequencies that are associated with the outer conscious levels.

Some authors advise that as you go to sleep at night, you think about your goals. That way, you get a little bit of alpha time for programming. The only trouble is, you have a tendency to fall asleep.

For now, I just want you to practice a simple exercise that will help you learn to enter and stay at the alpha level. Then, in forty days, you will be ready to begin your programming.

In the meantime, I will give you some additional tasks that you can perform at the beta level that will help you prepare yourself so that you will be able to program more effectively at the alpha level when you are ready at the completion of the forty days.

Your First Assignment

If you are using the Silva Centering Exercise (also known as the Long Relaxation Exercise) on the www.SilvaNow.com website to enter the alpha level, then you can skip the information that follows.

If you do not want to use the recording of the Silva Centering Exercise, and you have not attended a Silva seminar or used one of our home-study courses to learn to enter the alpha level, then you will need to follow the instructions here to learn to enter the alpha level on your own.

Here is your alpha exercise:

Practice this exercise in the morning when you first wake up. Since your brain is starting to shift from alpha to beta when you first wake up, you will not have a tendency to fall asleep when you enter alpha.

Here are the steps to take:

1. When you awake tomorrow morning, go to the bathroom if you have to, then go back to bed. Set your alarm clock to ring in fifteen minutes, just in case you do fall asleep again.

2. Close your eyes and turn them slightly upward toward your eyebrows (about 20 degrees). Research shows that this produces more alpha brain-wave activity.

3. Count backward slowly from 100 to 1. Do this silently; that is, do it mentally to yourself. Wait about one second between numbers.

4. When you reach the count of 1, hold a mental picture of yourself as a success. An easy way to do this is to recall the most recent time when you were 100 percent successful. Recall the setting, where you were and what the scene looked like; recall what you did; and recall what you felt like.

5. Repeat mentally, "Every day in every way I am getting better, better, and better."

6. Then say to yourself, "I am going to count from 1 to 5; when I reach the count of 5, I will open my eyes, feeling fine and in perfect health, feeling better than before."

7. Begin to count. When you reach 3, repeat, "When I reach the count of 5, I will open my eyes, feeling fine and in perfect health, feeling better than before."

8. Continue your count to 4 and 5. At the count of 5, open your eyes and tell yourself mentally, "I am wide awake, feeling fine and in perfect health, feeling better than before. And this is so."

These Eight Steps Are Really Only Three

Go over each of these eight steps so that you understand the purpose while at the same time become more familiar with the sequence.

1. The mind cannot relax deeply if the body is not relaxed. It is better to go to the bathroom and permit your body to enjoy full comfort. Also, when you first awake, you may not be fully awake. Going to the bathroom ensures your being fully awake. But in case you are still not awake enough to stay awake, set your alarm clock to ring in fifteen minutes so you do not risk being late on your daily schedule. Sit in a comfortable position.

2. Research has shown that when a person turns the eyes up about 20 degrees, it triggers more alpha rhythm in the brain and also causes more right-brain activity. Later, when we do our mental picturing, it will be with your eyes turned upward at this angle. Meanwhile, it is a simple way to encourage alpha brain-wave activity. You might want to think of the way you look up at the screen in a movie theater, a comfortable upward angle.

3. Counting backward is relaxing. Counting forward is activating. 1–2–3 is like "get ready, get set, go!" 3–2–1 is pacifying. You are going nowhere except deeper within yourself.

4. Imagining yourself the way you want to be—while relaxed— creates the picture. Failures who relax and imagine themselves making mistakes and losing frequently create a mental picture

that brings about failure. You will do the opposite. Your mental picture is one of success, and it will create what you desire: success.

5. Words repeated mentally—while relaxed—create the concepts they stand for. Pictures and words program the mind to make it so.

6–8. These last three steps are simply counting to 5 to end your session. Counting upward activates you, but it's still good to give yourself "orders" to become activated at the count of 5. Do this before you begin to count; do it again along the way; and again as you open your eyes.

Once you wake up tomorrow morning and prepare yourself for this exercise, it all works down to three steps:

1. Count backward from 100 to 1.
2. Imagine yourself successful.
3. Count yourself out 1 to 5, reminding yourself that you are wide awake, feeling fine, and in perfect health.

Forty Days That Can Change Your Life for the Better

You know what to do tomorrow morning, but what about after that? Here is your training program:

Count backward from 100 to 1 for 10 mornings.

Count backward from 50 to 1 for 10 mornings. Count backward from 25 to 1 for 10 mornings.

Count backward from 10 to 1 for 10 mornings.

After these 40 mornings of countdown relaxation practice, count backward only from 5 to 1 and begin to use your alpha level.

People have a tendency to be impatient, to want to move faster. Please resist this temptation and follow the instructions as written.

You must develop and acquire the ability to function consciously at alpha before the mental techniques will work properly for you. You must master the fundamentals first. We've been researching this field since 1944, longer than anyone else, and the techniques we have developed have helped millions of people worldwide to enjoy greater success and happiness, so please follow these simple instructions.

Appendix C

Contact Information and Additional Resources

FREE INTRODUCTORY LESSONS
www.SilvaNow.com

INFORMATION ABOUT SILVA COURSES AND PRODUCTS
www.SilvaCourses.com

To contact the authors of this book or any Silva UltraMind ESP Systems instructor, and for a schedule of seminars, please visit the Silva instructors' website: www.SilvaInstructors.com

SILVA INTERNATIONAL GRADUATE ASSOCIATION
www.SIGA.org

SILVA BOOKS, RECORDINGS, AND HOME-STUDY COURSES
www.SilvaCourses.com

ECUMENICAL SOCIETY HOLISTIC FAITH HEALING WEBSITE
www.ESPsy.org

JOSÉ SILVA JR.'S WEBSITE

www.SilvaJoseJr.com

KATHERINE SANDUSKY'S WEBSITE

www.SilvaSeminars.com

ED BERND JR., WITH AVLIS PUBLISHING AND AVLIS PRODUCTIONS INC.

www.SilvaCourses.com

DR. CLANCY D. MCKENZIE'S WEBSITE

www.alternativeapa.com

Index

CPSIA information can be obtained
at www.ICGtesting.com
Printed in the USA
JSHW060203230722
28305JS00003BA/3